BRISTOL FROM THE POST AND PRESS

MAURICE FELLS

AMBERLEY

ABOUT THE AUTHOR

Maurice Fells is a born and bred Bristolian who is passionate about his native city and its history, its people – past and present – and plans for its future.

As a journalist he has worked for the *Western Daily Press, Bristol Evening Post, HTV West* (now *ITV West*) and BBC West. He is a familiar voice on BBC Radio Bristol talking about local history matters.

First published 2017

Amberley Publishing
The Hill, Stroud
Gloucestershire, GL5 4EP

www.amberley-books.com

ISBN 978 1 4456 7120 8 (print)
ISBN 978 1 4456 7121 5 (ebook)

British Library Cataloguing in Publication Data. A catalogue record for this book is available from the British Library.

Origination by Amberley Publishing.
Printed in the UK.

CONTENTS

Acknowledgements   5
Introduction   6
1899: Royal Seal of Approval for Bristol   8
1921: Rugby Players Remembered   9
1925: Bristol Gets A New landmark   11
1932: Bristol Gets Its Own Paper   13
1932: 'We Will Remember Them'   15
1933: Archbishop Blesses Bristol   17
1938: The Daring Parachutist   18
1940: The Bristol Blitz   20
1941: VIPs Visit Bombed Areas   23
1941: Help for Blitz Victims   24
1942: Terror from the Sky   25
1944: The 'New Bristol'   27
1945: VE Day   28
1948: Zoo Death   31
1948: The Good Quads   32
1949: Lift-off for the Big 'BRAB'   33
1951: Major Oil Disaster   34
1954: Bristol Britannia Crashes   36
1955: How Bristol's Airport Took Off   37
1956: The Queen Opens New Council House   39
1956: A Right Royal Welcome for the Queen   42
1956: Flower of Bristol   43
1957: Britannia Crash Deaths   45
1957: Britannia Crash: Aircraft Firm's Statement   46
1958: ITV Comes West   46
1958: Pop Concert Chaos   47
1958: This Is Bristol Calling   50
1961: 'Fairest Church' under Threat   51
1962: A White Winter   53
1962: Road Chaos   54
1963: The First Lady   55
1963: The Beatles Make Their Bristol Debut   56
1964: Hotel Etiquette Rules   57
1964: The Beatles Are 'Flour-bombed'   59
1965: Road Improvements   60
1965: On Safari in Centre of Bristol   61
1965: Royal Service   62
1966: Government Attacks Church Show   63

1966: Swinging Sixties Hit Bristol 64
1966: Bridging the Severn Gap 65
1968: Cue Harlech 67
1969: Supersonic Flight 67
1969: Saving Maritime History 69
1970: SS *Great Britain* on the Move 70
1970: Back Home 70
1970: Home and Dry 72
1971: Avon Gorge 'Monster' 74
1971: Council Fashion 75
1972: Curtain Up at Oldest Theatre 76
1973: Second Cathedral for Bristol 77
1973: One of King Street's finest Returns 79
1973: Bristol 600 Celebrations 80
1974: Avon Calling Bristol 81
1977: Ships Ahoy! 82
1978: Cheers, Bristol 84
1978: World's First 'Test-tube Baby' 85
1979: Bridge Jumpers 86
1980: Riots 88
1981: Unexpected Royal Guest 89
1983: Hospital's Royal Visitor 90
1986: A University First 92
1989: University Bomb Attack 94
1994: Church History in the Making 95
1996: Firefighter Killed in Service 97
1996: Farewell Avon County 98
1996: End of a Television Era 98
1996: Ship Shape and Bristol Fashion 100
1996: A Second Severn Bridge 101
1997: Atlantic Voyage 102
1997: Journey's End 103
1999: Maundy Thursday Service 105
1999: Last Orders for Brewery 105
2000: The 'King of the Keyboard' 107
2003: Top Honour for MP 109
2003: Playground Peace 110
2007: Dockland Regeneration 111
2008: Retail Therapy 112
2012: Olympic Flame Arrives in Bristol 114
2012: First Directly Elected Mayor 117
2013: Rugby Club Trying for First Home Win 119
2015: Business and the Classroom 120
2016: Massive Concert 121
2016: Cycling City 123
2017: Concorde Gets A Home 125
2017: First Black Lord Lieutenant 126

ACKNOWLEDGEMENTS

As a journalist with a passion for all things Bristol it was a genuine labour of love to put this book together. However, it could not have been done without the help of others. I made numerous visits to the reference section of Bristol Central Library where the staff were most helpful and showed remarkable tolerance and patience in dealing with my enquiries. They were extremely helpful in guiding me through Bristol's daily newspapers going back more than a century, which are mostly on microfilm. Special thanks go to Dawn Dyer for her enthusiasm about this book and spending much time in searching out newspaper cuttings that were many years old and probably rarely looked at.

I must thank Janet and Trevor Naylor for their help, in so many ways, which ensured that *Bristol from the Post and Press* grew from an idea to a fully fledged book. Without their help, I'm sure this book would never have been completed.

INTRODUCTION

Have you heard about the day the Queen called into a pub for dinner completely unannounced? Or about the youth who jumped out of a plane for a dare? Or the woman who was expecting twins but gave birth to quadruplets and made history? Or the village that was destroyed to make way for the development of an aeroplane that the government scrapped after its maiden flight?

These and many other events in Bristol have been chronicled by newspapers since 1702 when William Bonny, a printer from London, settled in the city and published the *Bristol Post-Boy*. This was a single-sheet weekly publication and was one of the first provincial newspapers in the country. Bonny's paper carried the strapline 'An account of the most material news, both foreign and domestick'. It is believed that the *Post-Boy*, which Bonny not only printed but also edited, survived around thirteen years.

Since its demise the *Bristol Post-Boy* has had many successors. Some had only a brief existence of just a few months while ownership of others passed down the family line over the years; one man even started a paper while he was in Bristol's Newgate Prison serving a sentence for debt. Some newspapers supported a political party, others didn't but all had one thing in common: they were searching out and reporting the news in the area in which they circulated, being a mirror reflecting what was happening in their local patch.

The late eighteenth century saw the birth of evening papers and by 1908 Bristol had three evening as well as three morning papers including the *Western Daily Press*, which was founded in 1858 and is still published. Their journalists had a ringside seat reporting on events that were helping Bristol to become the thriving modern, vibrant city it is today. For a long time Bristol has been associated with national and international events.

The creation in 1932 of the *Bristol Evening Post* was a news story in itself. Indeed, the paper printed it and the story appears in this book. The new paper was published in opposition to the existing London-controlled *Evening World*. Both papers fought a tough circulation battle – known locally as the 'newspaper war' – until eventually the *World* was merged with the *Post*.

In 1960, the only remaining morning paper, the independently owned *Western Daily Press*, was on its economic knees and bought by the *Post*.

In cities where there were two evening papers competition was keen among rival reporters to make sure their particular publication was first with the news. There was rivalry, too, between the *Daily Press* and the *Post*, although they came from the same stable, and indeed shared the same newsroom. The morning paper published several county editions covering Bristol, Somerset, Gloucestershire and Wiltshire. Meanwhile, the *Post* printed three city and a number of country district editions each day from 11 a.m. onwards. All this meant that journalists could update breaking news edition by edition, as will be seen in this book. Very often the content of front pages would be changed between editions.

Both papers are published from the same building in Temple Way in the centre of the city, which was specially built in 1974 to cater for the 'new technology of the day'. The *Evening Post* editor told his readers in a front-page message that he and his staff would have to 'master the complexities of modern technology which would enable the paper to have larger pages'. With larger pages, he said, advertising would no longer 'dwarf the news'.

The *Evening Post* was not only reporting developments about the supersonic aircraft *Concorde*, being built by many of its readers at Filton, but also took part in a mission to America in a bid to persuade politicians there to admit Concorde to its skies. The paper also strenuously campaigned for the retention of grammar schools, and successfully fought for smear tests to be freely available as a safeguard against cervical cancer. Meanwhile, the *Western Daily Press* vigorously fought for expansion of the port of Bristol with the construction of Royal Portbury Dock, 8 miles downriver.

These were what 'old-school journalists' call the 'good old days of newspapers'. They said they would never be repeated and they haven't been.

Now that many evening papers, including the *Post*, have dropped the word 'evening' from their mastheads and their only printed edition is on sale in time to accompany the marmalade and toast at breakfast, breaking news can no longer be delivered through their pages. Instead, it comes through another 'new technology'; this time via the internet and the news websites and digital editions set up by the papers.

This book not only pays homage to the 'good old days of newspapers' but also to Bristol and its people. It aims to give the reader a flavour of the atmosphere of the city that often dares to be different through stories reported by the press and post. Besides featuring some of the good and the great there are stories that show Bristol's streak of independence and its quirky character. The book also looks back at the devastation the Second World War caused the city itself as well as the loss of life of its citizens.

There are stories too about the regeneration of the old city docks, how Bristol has become the cultural, shopping and entertainment capital of the West Country. There are also commentaries on royal visits and national sporting events held in the city. We begin though with the day that Bristol's first Lord Mayor was knighted by Queen Victoria, who carried out the investiture in the street without getting out of her carriage.

Maurice Fells, 2017

1899: ROYAL SEAL OF APPROVAL FOR BRISTOL

In spring 1899 the mayor of Bristol, Cllr Herbert Ashman, was told by the prime minister that 'the Queen has been pleased to direct that in future the Mayor of the City of Bristol shall have the style and title of Lord Mayor'. It meant that Mr Ashman was the last mayor and first Lord Mayor of Bristol. Later that year Queen Victoria knighted him. Rather unusually, the investiture took place outside the Council House in Corn Street. Queen Victoria did not even leave her carriage to knight Mr Ashman. The *Western Daily Press* devoted a whole broadsheet page to the royal visit. Its lengthy report included scores of names of civic dignitaries, details of their uniforms, what their ladies wore and information about the music played by the military bands along the royal route. The following paragraphs are taken from the report, which started with four headlines.

Western Daily Press, Thursday 16 November 1899

THE QUEEN IN BRISTOL
Great enthusiasm
Brilliant Pageant
The Lord Mayor Knighted

The arrival at Temple Meads
At 1.50 p.m. the train, drawn by the engine Badminton, made alongside the platform, and the carriage containing Her Majesty was stopped at the precise spot where arrangements had been made for the reception.

Many of those who accompanied the Royal party were early to alight, and when all had gathered around the Queen's carriage a slanting carpeted crimson board was fixed between the platform and compartment, down which Her Majesty walked leaning on the arm of an Indian attendant.

The Lord Mayor and Lady Mayoress were the first to be presented to the Queen by the Lord Chamberlain, and her Ladyship handed to the Queen a bouquet.

Her Majesty was soon seated in the Royal carriage drawn by four magnificent horses. The Princesses Christian and Henry of Battenberg and HRH the Duke of Connaught took their places with Her Majesty, and after their attendants looked after the Queen's comfort in adjusting her rug and cushions, the procession moved off at 2 o'clock.

The band outside the station played 'God Save The Queen' and the Royal carriage moved away. Soon from thousands of throats resounded cheer after cheer as the procession passed the crowds on its way to the Council House.

Ceremony at the Council House

The Council House in Bristol is situated in a narrow thoroughfare and space in Corn Street was contracted by the erection of a grandstand for the accommodation of members of the council and officers of the Corporation.

This structure was divided into two parts with places right and left of the entrance, and in the centre was a raised platform, covered with crimson cloth, running out beyond the stand for the accommodation of the Lord Mayor, the Recorder and Deputy Town Clerk who were concerned in the presentation of an address to the Queen, ex-Mayors and other gentlemen who were to be presented to Her Majesty. Under the circumstances referred to, the general public had not much opportunity of witnessing the ceremonial at the Council House for the whole roadway in Corn Street was reserved for the procession and Wine Street was occupied by the band of the 1st Gloucestershire Regiment under Bandmaster Webb who took up their positions by one o'clock and played patriotic airs during the period of waiting for the arrival of the Royal procession.

So far as the general public were concerned they had to be content with views of the proceedings from outside the Broad Street and Wine Street barriers. The time passed pleasantly, for every few minutes detachments of troops marched passed the stand and were saluted by the guard and cheered by spectators.

The Royal carriage drew up in front of the stand and Sir Arthur Biggs was observed to have unsheathed his sword and passed it to HRH Duke of Connaught who occupied the opposite seat to her Majesty in the Royal carriage.

The Queen then beckoned the Lord Mayor to kneel beside the carriage, and having received the sword from the Duke of Connaught held it above the Lord Mayor's head and bade him to rise as Sir Herbert Ashman. This was the signal for another round of cheering.

Another pleasing incident followed. When Her Majesty visited Bristol in 1830, Mr. W Mabey, a local musician, was a member of the band that played outside the hotel in The Mall at which the late Duchess of Kent and the Princess Victoria stayed.

Yesterday Mr. Mabey was stationed with the band of the Volunteer Battalion of the Gloucestershire Regiment in Wine Street, and he was presented to Her Majesty, and with that the proceedings at the Council House came to a close.

1921: RUGBY PLAYERS REMEMBERED

What might be termed the 'golden age of memorials' came after the end of the First World War. Most memorials were in the form of cenotaphs, plaques or statues but 300 local rugby footballers who lost their lives in the fighting between August 1914 and October 1918 are remembered by what must be Bristol's biggest memorial – the Memorial Stadium, which is dedicated to them. The ground, measuring

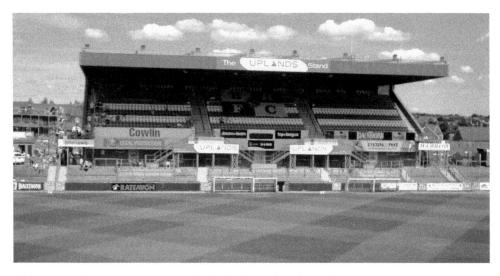

The Memorial Ground was originally built for rugby players but is now the home of Bristol Rovers FC. (Courtesy of Chris Clements under Creative Commons 3.0)

more than 6 acres, became the home of Bristol Rugby. However, since 1998 it has been the home of Bristol Rovers Football Club after the rugby club were in administration at the time. Launching an appeal for funds to build the original rugby stadium, the Lord Mayor Mr J. T. Francombe wrote a special message to the readers of the *Western Daily Press*.

Western Daily Press, Monday 11 July 1921

BRISTOL RUGBY GROUND

As one of the consequences of the late war there is no ground in or near the city at the present time suitable or available for a first-class rugby match.

The position was fully discussed at a meeting held at the Council House recently, and it was resolved to start a fund for the purpose of purchasing and equipping a ground as a memorial to the three hundred local rugby footballers who fell in the war, the same to be vested in trustees for the use of the Bristol Football Club as the representative city XV, and as the headquarters of the rugby game.

The influence of sport and the part played by the young men of the country in the last war has never been sufficiently appreciated nor recognised, and it was felt that in Bristol there could be no finer memorial to those who gave their lives to their country's cause or a more fitting mark of appreciation of those who fought and returned home, than the provision of such a ground.

This appeal is directed more particularly to those who, from various causes, had not the privilege of serving in a Naval or Military capacity during the late crisis, but it is hoped that it will also have the genuine support of all those who have the interest of the rugby game at heart.

A suitable plot of ground at Horfield, adjacent to the tram route, and covering six and a half acres, has already been purchased, and it is estimated that a sum of

£10,000 will be required to drain, level and properly equip the same with stands, dressing rooms and the usual accommodation for players and spectators.

Bristol Memorial Ground was officially opened by the Lord Mayor in 1921. Immediately after the opening ceremony the first match kicked off with Bristol beating Cardiff 18 points to three. Bristol Rugby now shares Ashton Gate stadium with Bristol City FC.

1925: BRISTOL GETS A NEW LANDMARK

Construction work on the Wills Memorial Building started in 1914 but was interrupted by the First World War and was not completed until 1925. However, the eleven-year wait was worthwhile as Bristol got a neo-Gothic 215-foot-high landmark tower, which was opened by George V and Queen Mary. The tower, part of Bristol University campus, was built by brothers Sir George and Mr Henry Herbert Wills as a monument to their father Henry Overton Wills, who endowed the university in 1909

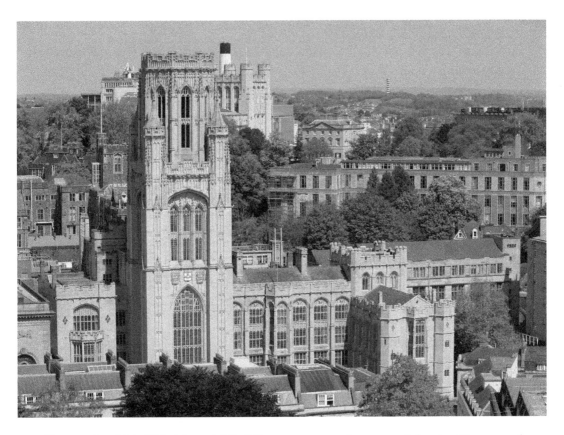

The 215-foot-high Wills Memorial Building towers over the centre of the city. (Courtesy of Rodw under Creative Commons 3.0)

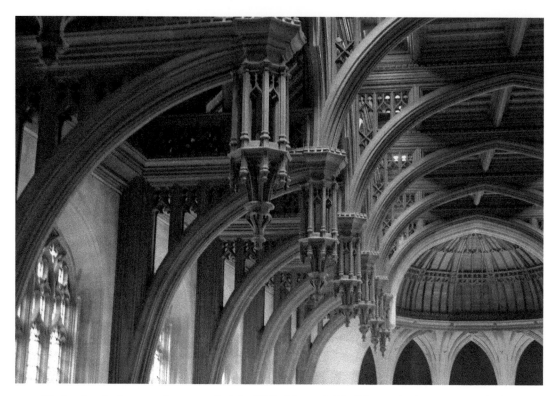

Timber for the hammer beam roof of the Wills Memorial Building, which was restored after the Second World War, came from an estate in Gloucestershire. (Courtesy of Bristollcarus under Creative Commons 3.0)

with £100,000. The *Western Daily Press* devoted several broadsheet pages to the royal opening with many details about academic and civic dignitaries at the ceremony. The report began with an overview of the day's proceedings.

Western Daily Press, Wednesday 10 June 1925

BRISTOL'S WELCOME TO KING AND QUEEN
Historic ceremony at university

Glorious weather favoured the Royal visit to Bristol yesterday and their majesties were enthusiastically greeted by dense crowds with citizens assembled along the comparatively short line of route.

At the Council House the King acknowledged an address of welcome from the corporation and after luncheon at the Victoria Rooms both the King and Queen shook hands with the local centenarian 'Little' Jackie Legge (the crippled son of a Mons hero) who wore his father's medals.

The real object of the Royal visit was the opening of the new building at the university and here the King replied to two addresses – one from the university and another from the Society of Merchant Venturers. His Majesty said the founder of the

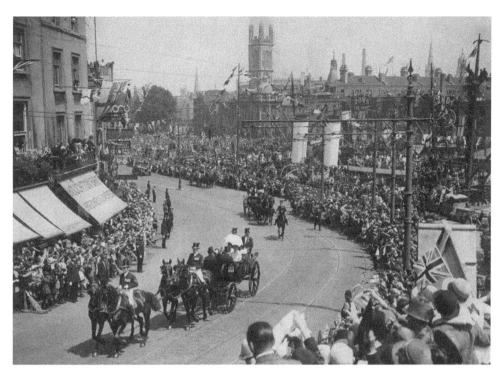

Thousands of people lined the streets as King George V and Queen Mary made their way to the Wills Memorial Building.

university has left an inspiring example of unremitting devotion to a high ideal and his share in that noble family memorial would ever be gratefully remembered.

At the end of the day the King described the visit as 'very successful' though it had been 'very hot'. The Queen remarked that everything had gone off 'splendidly'.

1932: BRISTOL GETS ITS OWN PAPER

In the late 1920s and early 1930s, there was strong feeling in Bristol that it should have its own newspaper instead of the *Evening World*, which was owned by London's newspaper barons. So twelve local businessmen became directors and hundreds of Bristolians invested in £1 shares to create the *Bristol Evening Post*. The first edition, carrying the front-page slogan 'The Paper You Have So Eagerly Awaited', rolled off the presses on 18 April 1932. A remarkable 138, 529 copies were sold that day, a number that every provincial editor must envy today with circulations plunging and papers all over the country closing.

A circulation 'war' broke out between the two papers. Eventually the *Evening World* merged with the *Evening Post*, which also bought the city's independent morning paper, the *Western Daily Press*. Today the *Bristol Evening Post* is known as the *Bristol Post*.

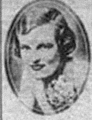
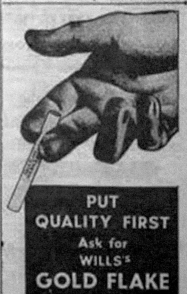
The first edition of the *Bristol Evening Post*. (Photo credit: Trevor Naylor)

Bristol Evening Post, Monday 18 April 1932

BRISTOL'S HAPPY WELCOME TO THE EVENING POST
Extraordinary scenes of enthusiasm in city streets

The Evening Post was born at 2 o'clock today, and Bristol showed itself a very proud parent.

Its welcome was all that we hoped and believed it would be.

A crowd had been waiting outside our office in Silver Street for hours in anticipation of the event.

Excitement grew with the passing of the dinner-hour, and at 2 o'clock, with the clang of the warning bell in the machine room, the giant presses, from a soft purr gradually raised their voices to a roar.

Soon the newsboys came dashing out with huge bundles of papers under their arms.

They had not gone a few paces before they were mobbed by eager customers and they had not gone a dozen paces from the office before they had to return for fresh supplies.

Meanwhile, the yellow *Evening Post* vans pulled out from their line and sped away to the outskirts of the city.

The Evening Post was launched!

So eager were buyers of first copies that no change was asked for.

'When are they coming out?' was the remark one frequently heard during the lunch-hour at Tramway Centre.

'Here is sixpence. Send me one of the papers as I cannot miss my train.'

Such was the message given to a Post reporter when he was standing at Tramway Centre by a Bristolian when dashing for a tram-car to take him to Temple Meads for his train to London.

When the newsboys arrived at Tramway Centre they were simply besieged, the papers going like hot cakes.

Passengers left tram cars – boarding the next one – to get a *Post*.

One seller had to execute a big order, selling 30 copies to one buyer.

And on every pavement were small groups of men and women running through the pages eagerly searching for their old favourites, and by the smiles on their faces, found them.

The president of the Bristol Rotary Club (Mr. R. T. Stoddard) at the luncheon today welcomed the representative of the *Evening Post* for the first time, amid hearty applause.

1932: 'WE WILL REMEMBER THEM'

While most towns and cities unveiled their civic war memorials a couple of years or so after the end of the First World War, Bristolians had to wait while council officials argued about the cost, its style and its location. Eventually, a competition was held to find a suitable design. It was fourteen years after the war ended that Field Marshall Sir William Birdwood, an 'old boy' of Clifton College, Bristol, unveiled the Cenotaph, similar to the one in Whitehall. Bristol had sent out around 55,000 men to the Western

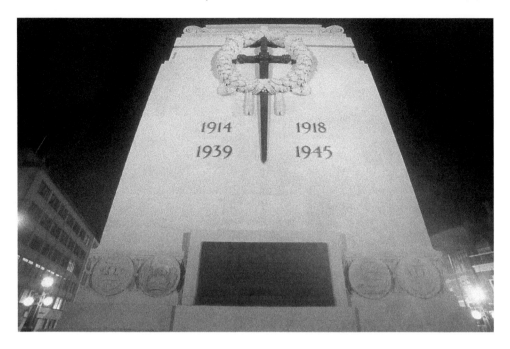

Bristol's Cenotaph was erected in memory of servicemen killed in the First World War. The reference to the Second World War was added later. (Courtesy of Rob Brewer under Creative Commons 3.0)

Front but around 6,000 of them never returned. The *Evening Post* devoted the best part of a page to the unveiling ceremony. These extracts are taken from it:

Bristol Evening Post, Monday 27 June 1932

TENS OF THOUSANDS SEE CENOTAPH UNVEILED

In the presence of 50,000 of their citizens, representatives of every class, Bristol's war memorial, a cenotaph, was unveiled by Field Marshall Sir William Birdwood.

Wonderful have been year after year Bristol's Armistice Day services, yesterday's ceremony surpassed them as an act of reverent remembrance.

There was less of the sense of poignancy of grief, rather a sense of satisfaction that at last there was a permanent memorial to the 6,000 gallant men and some few no less gallant women of Bristol who lived worthy of the traditions of their city and country even unto death.

The report later spoke of the crowds who gathered around the Cenotaph. 'One could not have wished a more fitting ceremony. The great crowd, gathered in from every part of the city, sensed the solemnity of the occasion. Voices were hushed. There was no commotion as they took their places, men, women and children, around the enclosure where the memorial stood with shrouds.

They filled not only the streets but every available window overlooking the memorial. They thronged on the roofs of buildings and gathered on the top of St Stephen's church tower.

After listing the various clergy taking part in the ceremony and naming the numerous uniformed military service units lined up in Colston Avenue facing the memorial, the newspaper report described the unveiling itself.

All religious denominations shared in the service. The singing of Kipling's 'Recessional' preceded the unveiling ceremony by Field Marshall Sir William Birdwood, who wore khaki uniform, his breast covered with four decks of service ribbons. As he pulled the chords that freed the shrouds covering the memorial it was disclosed with the golden sword and Union Jacks surrounding it. The troops presented arms and buglers sounded the Last Post and Reveille.

Sir William Birdwood speaking in a clear voice that could be heard throughout the park through the amplifiers, in an eloquent address that had special appeal because of his close association with Bristol, said: 'It was the spirit of sacrifice which animated those Bristol citizens, officers and men to pay the supreme price for which the monument memorial has been erected.'

1933: ARCHBISHOP BLESSES BRISTOL

The people of Bristol could not have seen a church service of such pomp and pageantry as this for many a year. The Archbishop of Canterbury, Dr Cosmo Lang, presided over a service of thanksgiving marking the completion of the fourth 'Great Restoration' of St Mary Redcliffe Church. Dr Lang was joined in procession by more than forty clergy, including eight bishops and former vicars of Redcliffe. After preaching the sermon, Dr Lang offered the 'Great Prayer of Hallowing' by candlelight. Then he went to the steps of Redcliffe's north porch and pronounced his blessing upon Bristol. He was watched by thousands of people who could not gain entry to the church but had waited several hours outside on a cold night to see him.

Western Daily Press, Saturday 4 November 1933

HALLOWED DAY IN 600 HISTORIC YEARS
Primate at Great Redcliffe Ceremony
Moving scene at Blessing of City

In moments of unutterable solemnity, with the whole church clothed in darkness save for the flood-lights filtering through the highest windows and the dim radiance of the candles at the altar, the fourth and greatest restoration of St. Mary Redcliffe Church, Bristol, was hallowed by the Archbishop of Canterbury at the great service of thanksgiving last night.

The hallowing of the restored glory of the Queen of the West was the climax of an occasion such as few generations are privileged to see, and which for its significance, colourful spectacle and deep sincerity will never be forgotten by the thousands who took part in it.

The service celebrated the three years' restoration scheme, which cost nearly £100,000.

In his sermon to a congregation of 1,300 people, the Primate said: 'Whoever enters this glorious church, as I did a short time ago, if he have any soul within him, must needs be stirred by a profound emotion.

He will at once realise the truth of those words familiar to Bristol people that he is beholding the fairest, the goodliest and most famous parish church in all England.

He will see stretched before him so very perfectly the power of our old English Gothic architecture abiding fresh and fair after a lapse of 350 years.

The sight is enough to make him catch his breath and feel a sense of mingled awe and joy.

Yet only three years ago there came all over this loveliness the shadow of a sudden fear.

It was reported on an authority that could not be questioned, that unless, so it was then computed, £60,000 could be found at once nothing could save these stones from perishing and decaying.

How could anyone who knows the church rest in peace with that knowledge?

Yet how in these days of strain and difficulty could a sum so large be raised?

Then it was that a worthy citizen of Bristol, true to the great traditions of merchants such as William Canynges and many others whose pride it was to adorn this church, conceived the noble ambition that he might himself restore his glorious church whatever the cost might be.

Today he sees his ambition fulfilled.

Let me say a few words to the worshippers of Redcliffe. I know your pride and deep sense of gratification for the generosity which has restored your church, but do not let your familiarity with the beauty of your church make you heedless of the responsibility that beauty lays on you'.

After the service, the Archbishop, wearing his mitre and cope of gold and white, moved alone to the North Porch and before a great gathering of people pronounced his blessing upon Bristol, the scene being one of striking beauty and solemnity.

He emerged into a glare of floodlights and magnesium flares and faced a battery of press cameras and gave his blessing 'on the parish, the port, the city and the diocese'.

Police were called out to deal with the crowds held spellbound by the wonder of the floodlit fabric of the church.

1938: THE DARING PARACHUTIST

Hundreds of people were shocked to see a man jump from a plane flying over the Avon Gorge and eventually land on a rooftop in Clifton. But the man himself showed no concern for his safety – for he was carrying out a dare. The next day he explained to an *Evening Post* reporter why he had done it:

Bristol Evening Post, Friday 3 June 1938

BRISTOL YOUTH WHO JUMPED FROM PLANE
'I should like to have come down in the Centre of Bristol'

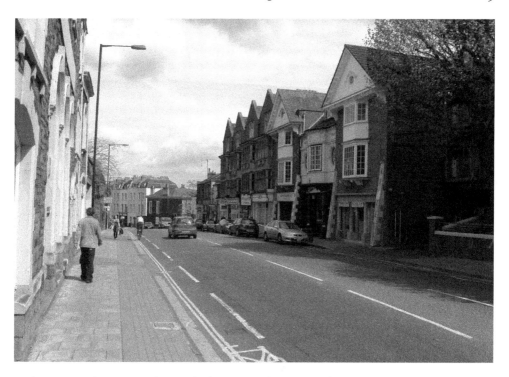

Park Row, in the centre of Bristol, the scene of an unusual parachute drop. (Courtesy of Repton1x under Creative Commons 3.0)

Thousands of people saw Albert Gourd, aged 17, of Easton Road, Easton, leap from an aeroplane, which was flying high above the Avon Gorge last night. At first they could only identify what looked like a black object falling from the machine.

It dropped sheer for some hundreds of feet then the parachute opened and they saw suspended from it a man.

In the strong breeze he was carried quickly over the city.

Motorists dashed off in pursuit and saw him dropping towards the university.

Suddenly he seemed to swoop downwards and was lost to sight.

People in Park Row and neighbourhood saw the parachute entangled in the chimney stack of No. 86 and the parachutist hanging by the ropes at the side of the house.

By wonderful good fortune he found a foothold on the snow box of the water pipe leading down from the roof, and thus took the weight of the fabric of the parachute.

Someone with ready wit found a builder's ladder at the university science wing extensions at the top of Woodland Road. Ready hands assisted in hurrying it to the scene.

The parachutist showing amazing unconcern grasped the rungs, swung round it and descended to the ground, undamaged beyond a scratch on the leg and bruised ribs.

So little was he hurt, that he at once climbed the ladder to the roof to disentangle his parachute from the chimney. Then he lit a cigarette without as much as a tremor.

Now let Mr. Gourd who is engaged in the building trade but is also in the Reserve of the 501 Bombing Squadron, whose school is at Filton, continue his story.

'I was flying in a Hawker Hart, piloted by Flying Officer Rayner, and occupying the air gunner's seat.

There was nothing the matter with the aeroplane when I jumped and I did it for bravado.

The pilot did not know anything about it, you bet. I had previously told people that I was going to do it, and they were constantly picking me up that I had not done it.

I had only been up once before and then only for five minutes. This time I had been in the air exactly four minutes.

When I jumped I decided that before I pulled the parachute cord I was going to count three but I think I counted two very slowly. I was falling at a rate of 120 feet a second so I should have fallen about 240 feet when I pulled the cord.

Nothing happened for a moment and I got the usual feeling of 'will it, or won't it'. I kept falling and then it opened with a terrific jerk, almost like breaking every bone in my body and I am still covered with bruises from the harness.

I was not scared. In fact I have never been scared of anything that I can remember except having two teeth out. I was glad to pass over the Avon clear of the mud and I was very thankful to pass several rather sharp steeples. I fell very fast for the 'chute opened as the wind was so strong. Immediately the pilot missed me he made for the drome, and lorries were soon searching for me.

After all, one does value one's life, even if one does not mind getting knocked about a bit, as I do not.

My nickname among my pals is 'Dare' because I am usually ready to dare anything and have been in hospital several times as the result of my escapades.

The possibility of my getting knocked down, if I landed, as I hoped somewhere in the centre of the city did not worry me because I am usually ready to dare any overhead electricity wires.

I felt it was no good coming down in a field - somewhere safe and easy – because anybody could do that'.

The pilot of the plane reported when he got back to Filton that he was not aware that a passenger had left the plane until he felt its balance disturbed.

Albert Gourd's mother said: 'Two RAF officers called at the house and informed us that our son had made the jump and was missing. It was such a shock to me – he is our only son – and I have not recovered from it yet.

But when the officers were still here we were asked to go to the telephone by a neighbour and we then heard to our joy that our son had landed safely.

Of course he did a foolish thing last night but he must have been very plucky'.

1940: THE BRISTOL BLITZ

One of the worst German air raids during the Bristol Blitz happened on 24 November 1940. It started at about 6.30 p.m. with the 'All Clear' being sounded around midnight. During those six hours many churches, public buildings and the city's main shopping centre were reduced to rubble. The face of Bristol would never be the same again. There were so many fires that seventy-seven fire brigades from across the country were called in to help. In this one raid alone 207 people lost their lives. Another 187 people were seriously injured and a further 703 slightly hurt. Wartime censorship meant that

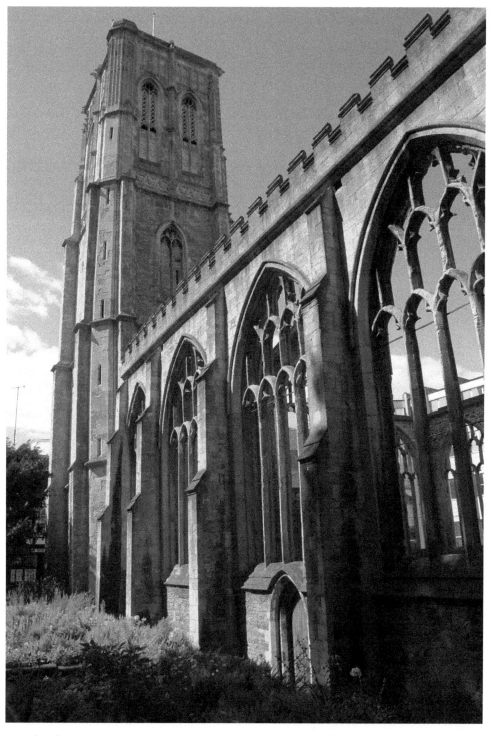

Temple Church, Temple Way, was one of eighteen Church of England buildings in Bristol destroyed during the Second World War. Its ruins still stand. (Courtesy of Ulli11015 under Creative Commons 3.0)

sometimes raids were not directly reported in the press. Vague stories, for example about a 'Town in the West', often appeared.

Bristol Evening Post, Monday 26 November 1940

GERMANS CONCENTRATE ON WEST TOWN
Churches, Theatre, Cinemas, Schools, Home for Aged, Historic Buildings, Shopping and Commercial Property Damaged
Heroic Work by Fire Fighting and ARP Services

The enemy's main attack last night was aimed at a town in the West of England. It began soon after darkness and continued till shortly before midnight. Some persons were killed and others injured.

Relays of raiders were active for several hours. A home for elderly people, at least half a dozen places of worship, a school, a theatre, cinemas, shops, houses and commercial buildings suffered damage by fire and blast.

A grammar school, a warehouse, and coal yards were also affected. At least 50 fires were burning at one time.

The raiders, flying singly and almost continuously, were facing challenges by anti-aircraft batteries.

Townspeople remained calmed throughout the raid and afterwards toured some streets to see the damage.

In the next morning when men, women and girls streamed to their places of business, the same calm and courage continued to show.

'I'm tough' declared one girl and certainly that was the quality shown by everyone.

Shopping centres suffered severely as did some perfect specimens of ancient and modern architecture and places of historic interest.

Bombs also fell in several thoroughfares. Having regard to the scale of the attack the casualties were remarkably light.

The call on the firemen – regular and auxiliary – was responded to with the greatest gallantry, and assistance was rushed in from neighbouring areas.

But it would be better to say that not only the firefighting services but all the air raid defence services worked heroically.

Working coolly and without pause unstinted admiration was granted them everywhere.

A part-time auxiliary fireman was killed when bombs exploded while he was working at the height of the attack.

Two young men and a woman reporter at offices in the same building, seeking to escape by the back garden door – the front being ablaze – found it locked.

With bombs falling around them they broke it with a pick and spade ensuring the escape of the other people in the premises only just in time.

A milk bar opened at the height of the attack and although buildings on each side were in flames the employees handed out soup to the firemen and ARP workers.

Landmarks on high ground were outlined by the light of flames. The tower of a church loomed up through the smoke and flames and several industrial buildings were shown up in silhouette.

Particularly good work was done by firemen in preventing the spread of a fierce blaze to a big block of adjacent buildings.

1941: VIPS VISIT BOMBED AREAS

Many eminent people including King George and Queen Mary and Prime Minister Winston Churchill visited Bristol during the war to see the damage and offer their sympathy to the citizens. On the morning after what became known as the 'Good Friday' Blitz, in which 180 people lost their lives, Mr Churchill was in Bristol for a congregation of the University of Bristol in his role as its chancellor. The ceremony had to be moved from the university's Great Hall, which had been extensively damaged in the air raid, to another room.

Bristol Evening Post, Saturday 12 April 1941

SAVAGE NAZI ONSLAUGHT ON BRISTOL

Bristol was savagely attacked last night by wave upon wave of German bombers.

Churches, a hospital, a school, two cinemas, a district library and commercial premises and houses suffered damage.

Firemen, street fire parties, and other services fought flames and incendiaries continuously, and their gallant and professional response to every call saved much property and life.

Mr. Winston Churchill saw much of the destruction in this and previous raids during a visit which he paid to the city today.

The Prime Minister with the American Ambassador and President Roosevelt's direct representative in connection with the Lease-and-Lend Act today toured some of Bristol's blitzed areas.

Mr. Churchill, complete with familiar hat and inevitable cigar, left his hotel early today and met the Lord Mayor and Town Clerk at the Council House.

When the distinguished visitors and civic officials began their tour, the news spread quickly and cheering crowds soon gathered.

Smiling broadly and standing in an open car, the Prime Minister waved his hat and cigar in acknowledgement.

He looked very fit and discussed Bristol's ordeal with members of the official party.

Just as his car turned out of sight, a large crowd of men and women came running towards the Council House waving and cheering breathlessly as accompanying cars started off in its wake.

In the blitzed areas he was also heartily cheered by people who endured a severe ordeal last night. He replied 'God bless you'.

To a man working on repairs on a bombed building, Mr. Churchill said: 'Don't worry. We will give it them back.'

At a place where shelter building was in progress he told the bricklayers: 'I've done a bit of that' a reference to the time when he made bricklaying a hobby.

Among those with whom he talked in a residential area was a woman whose house suffered last night.

Mr. Churchill held out his hand but she demurred because her hand was dirty from 'cleaning up'. But the Prime Minister insisted on shaking hands.

Mr. Churchill bought from a sailor one of the emblems – a Union Jack – on sale in aid of Bristol's Own Fund for providing comfort for men in the Services and Civil Defence.

One of the objects of Mr. Churchill's visit was to attend the Congregation for the Conferment of Degrees at Bristol University, of which he is Chancellor.

The Congregation was a special one for the conferment of an honorary degree of Doctor of Laws on Mr. Menzies, Prime Minister of Australia.

With Mr. Churchill were his wife and their daughter Mary.

The party arrived in the early hours after the blitz and had breakfast at the Grand Hotel.

1941: HELP FOR BLITZ VICTIMS

With bombardment following bombardment, it was no surprise that many families were having sleepless nights or suffering from fatigue and depression. The city council came up with the idea of providing mothers and children with the chance to get away from it all.

Western Daily Press, Saturday 26 April 1941

REST PERIODS FOR BRISTOLIANS

Hundreds of Bristol mothers and children who have suffered from the horrors of the savage Nazi bombardment on our city are to be sent away to the country and seaside for rest periods from two to three weeks.

Preliminary details of the scheme were given to the *Western Daily Press* by the Lord Mayor, Alderman T. Underdown, who spoke of the concern of the Emergency and War Appeals Committees for the needs of 'Blitzed' mothers and children in the matter of a holiday, and their intention is to go ahead with their plans immediately.

'It is hoped to secure hundreds of billets in country and seaside places in the West Country' said the Lord Mayor 'and plans are going ahead rapidly for a great holiday camp on a well-known West Country estate, which will be opened about mid-May and will carry on until mid-September.

Our most urgent need in connection with the camp is for beds of all kinds, and we should be most grateful for offers of help in this respect.'

Once the scheme has got into its stride we hope to send away hundreds of women and children every week for a complete rest for two or three weeks. So far as the billets are concerned, the holidays will commence within a day or two for a party of 40 to 50 mothers and children.

'The first party will be going to a Devon resort, this particular town having been magnificent to us in offering free hospitality in practically every case. On behalf of the citizens of Bristol I should like to say how very grateful we are to the people there for their initiative in making this wonderful gesture of goodwill and sympathy towards the 'blitzed' people of our city'.

This holiday scheme will be financed by the Lord Mayor's Services Fund, and a central office for the enrolment of the mothers and children has been set up by the Medical Officer Dr. R. H. Parry.

Mr. H. V. Hindle, secretary of the Lord Mayor's War Services Council, said the city authorities had tackled the problem on the widest possible scale. They wanted the mothers and children, wherever possible, to get away to peaceful and quiet surroundings for a couple of weeks or so to recoup their strength after the horrors of bombardment and the general strain of war conditions.

1942: TERROR FROM THE SKY

The single most serious incident in Bristol during the Second World War happened at the end of a morning rush hour when completely unannounced a bomb fell in busy Broad Weir in the centre of the city. It fell at a spot where three buses were standing. In this air raid forty-five people were killed and another forty-five injured. Altogether during the war 1,299 people lost their lives and another 3,305 were injured.

Bristol Evening Post, Friday 28 August 1942

BOMB FALLS AMID 3 BUSES IN BRISTOL

Two raiders came in high and dropped a bomb on Bristol this morning.

The bomb fell at a junction where three buses laden with business people were halted. The casualty list will probably be heavy.

The bomb fell amid the buses, and in a moment two were afire, the occupants being trapped; the other was wrecked. A number of people passing in the street were blown a considerable distance by the blast.

A 16th century timber building which was the home of an old-established printing firm, partially collapsed, while an adjacent building on the street corner was brought down completely.

It is feared that a number of people are beneath the debris. Ambulances were quickly on the scene, and those of the injured who could be extricated were removed to hospital.

It happened that the normal terminus for the buses had been transferred to allow street alterations, and this accounted for there being three of them at the spot, while, happening at an hour when traffic was heavy, the sufferers greater in number than would have been the case at other than the peak hour of morning travel.

The bomb came absolutely without warning so that nobody had time to take shelter. The buses were a mass of flames almost immediately the bomb burst, and nothing could be done for the people within. Though the fire brigades were on the spot of the fire within little more than a minute, they could do little except prevent the spread of the fire to nearby buildings.

Even when the firemen were playing hoses on the burning debris of the building which had collapsed, others were tearing away beams and broken woodwork in the seemingly vain hope of rescuing workers believed to have been on the premises.

For a wide area around there was considerable damage to property and many shop windows were broken.

A press photographer had a lucky escape. He had been on fire-watching duty overnight and as he was leaving his office to go home a bus passed him. He ran to catch it but was just too late. That bus was involved in the tragedy.

As the bus passed out of sight round a corner he heard the sound of the plane overhead, followed almost immediately by the unmistakable shriek of the falling bomb.

It crashed through into a culvert close to the nearest bus, while a second bus just ahead of it caught the full blast. The third bus, outward bound, was wrecked but did not catch fire. People, seriously injured and some dead, were lying on the road, among them women and children.

It is believed that the drivers and conductors of two of the buses were among the dead.

Aboard one of the buses, in which a baby was among the victims, everybody was a casualty with the exception of the conductress, who escaped with shock. Her first thought was for the driver. 'Is my driver safe?' she asked again and again.

The enemy aircraft, hotly pursued by gunfire, quickly made off in a south-easterly direction.

An eye-witness was Mr. H. Sheppard, who keeps a shop close by. He said: 'There was a girl on the rear platform on one of the burning buses, and with another man I rushed up and caught hold of her – but as the flames swept up we had to release our hold. The heat was too intense for anyone to be able to do anything.

Another young woman who jumped from the top of a bus, was caught by bystanders, and I believe was uninjured'.

An old lady of 93, known to neighbours as 'Granny Horne,' was trapped in her sitting room by fallen masonry. A woman living nearby talked and waved to Granny Horne to keep her spirits up while for nearly an hour the rescue squad was working hard to release her.

She remained cheerful throughout and suffered only mild shock. When asked if she had any water handy she replied with a bright smile: 'Yes, but I want that to wash out the milk bottles!'

Group Warden P. J. Pollock paid a tribute to the splendid work of Deputy Group Warden Miss Elsie Cottrell, who was in charge of the local post when the bomb fell.

Mr. Pollock said: 'When I arrived, Miss Cottrell was carrying on with the work at the post as though at practice. The whole personnel, including the nurses and the boy messengers, carried out their duties just like the drill book.

The messengers have been of the greatest assistance in many ways, and have been particularly useful in reporting incidents to the police. They are only young, but with their faces blackened, they have gone about their duties most efficiently'.

Tributes were also paid to the work of three ladies of the Church Army who were quickly on the spot with a mobile canteen. Mrs Wharton, the matron and the Misses Cox dispensed 50 gallons of tea to rescue parties.

Rescue parties were still hard at work this afternoon, digging amid the ruins of a small fruiterer's shop which had completely collapsed.

It was feared that the shopkeeper, an elderly man named Herring, was buried with the fall of the building. He was known to have been in the premises shortly before.

It is feared that at least three council school children who habitually catch one of the buses involved in the tragedy may be among the victims.

1944: THE 'NEW BRISTOL'

During the war more than 3,000 houses were destroyed across the city while nearly 100,000 properties were damaged. The whole area, which is now Castle Park in the centre of the city, was reduced to rubble, including the city's popular shopping centre. Beaten but not bowed, the city planners wasted no time in taking on the massive task of designing a 'new Bristol'.

Bristol Evening Post, Wednesday 15 March 1944

NEW BRISTOL: FULL PLANS OF TRANSFORMATION
Changing heart of the city

The secret is out today. We know the vision of the Bristol which is seen through the eyes of the city's Planning and Reconstruction Committee.

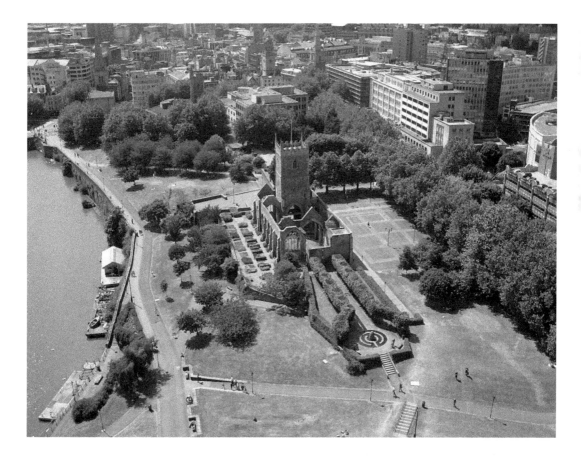

Castle Park was developed on the site of Bristol's main shopping centre, destroyed in the Second World War. The bombed remains of St Peter's Church still stand. (Couresy of Arpingstone under the Creative Commons 3.0)

It is bold beyond the wildest dreams of most people, but it is conceived through the telescope of fifty years ahead – to meet the needs of the Bristol of 2000 AD.

This, of course, does not mean that the work will not commence immediately the government says 'Go'.

But what the cost will be no one can tell nor, as far as we can see, has it been considered.

From the plans it would appear to have been designed on what is regarded as desirable, regardless of other considerations.

The chief interest probably lies in the future of the main shopping centre in the city.

As foreshadowed in the *Evening Post* the reconstruction visualises its transfer en bloc from the old Wine Street/Castle Street site to a new area circled roughly around Merchant Street and occupied by 35 acres.

The plateau from High Street to Old Market Street, including the site of the old Bristol Castle, will be laid out as a public park, extending down to Fairfax Street and Broad Weir.

Bridge Street and what was Back Bridge Street will be included in a new artery road from Bristol Bridge to Old Market Street, linking up with Baldwin Street.

The central park area will be carried across the river to Bath Street, which would mean the removal of George's Brewery if carried out.

As for the shopping centre it will be circular in shape with arcaded shops, and the surrounding area consisting of large blocks built to the most modern and approved description without necessarily being uniform to the degree of monotony.

No through roads are envisaged but back service roads are provided for receipt and dispatch of goods.

One of the outstanding proposals is the creation of a university medical training centre occupying the whole of the rising land from Upper Maudlin Street to Kingsdown Parade and then to St. Michael's Park.

This will virtually bring the Eye Hospital, Dental Hospital and Royal Infirmary into unity with the Maternity Hospital, Children's Hospital and the university building at the crown of the eminence.

The Lewins Mead area below Upper Maudlin Street is seen as the site of a great bus station.

1945: VE DAY

A sense of relief fell over Bristol, like the rest of the country, as the news gradually spread that the formal act of military surrender had been signed by Germany, thus ending the war in Europe. Prime Minister Churchill declared in a radio broadcast that 8 May would be a public holiday in Britain, known as Victory in Europe Day. In Bristol there were hastily organised street parties in almost every suburb with impromptu community singing on many a street corner. The Lord Mayor travelled around various parts of the

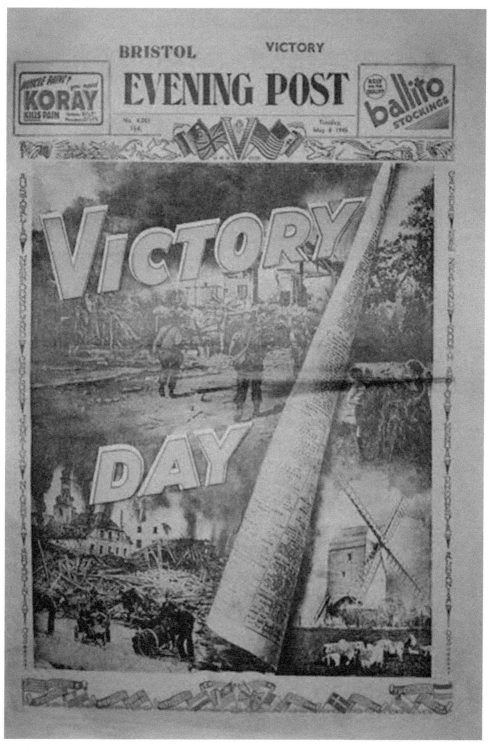

Evening Post VE Day edition. (Photo credit: Trevor Naylor.)

city in the horse-drawn proclamation coach to make the official announcement that war was over. The *Bristol Evening Post* published a special 'Victory Edition':

Bristol Evening Post, Tuesday 8 May 1945

CROWD'S ROAR OF CHEERING
Bristol celebrates

From the historic Proclamation Coach the Lord Mayor this afternoon addressed a crowd of citizens numbering several thousand and stretching a long distance in every direction outside the Council House. Many of them brought flags.

The Prime Minister's broadcast speech – that hostilities will cease at one minute after midnight – was relayed to the assembly by means of amplifiers.

The crowd were entertained while waiting by amplified music, and many joined in singing popular refrains.

The Lord Mayor, in his scarlet and ermine robes, was accompanied by the Sheriff and by the City Swordbearer. Nearby were former Lord Mayors and civic officials. The Lady Mayoress was at the ceremony.

The Lord Mayor, who began by saying, 'The great day has arrived' said they were gathered together in great heart, and in thankfulness for the complete victory in Europe which had been achieved, thanks to our gallant fighting forces.

It was an occasion for rejoicing and it was right that we should do so. After that we must gird ourselves and finish the Japanese War as speedily as possible.

The scene was truly worthy of the great occasion – colourful, joyful and impressive.

There was a great cheer when the Proclamation Coach, surmounted by its red coronet, drove up to the Council House, and as soon as it passed, the crowd broke through the police cordon and surged forward behind it. It was the first occasion the carriage had been used since King George VI was proclaimed.

A flag seller did a roaring trade, although almost everyone already had patriotic favours of some kind.

The civic party were greeted with a roar of applause, to be followed by a great hush as the chimes of Big Ben came over the loudspeakers.

A murmur of applause and some clapping came when the Premier spoke of the liberation of the Channel Islands, and another outburst of applause as he finished.

The crowd who had previously sung the National Anthem with great fervour, gave lusty cheers – led by the Lord Mayor – for the King, the Prime Minister and the Fighting Services.

Later the Lord Mayor, with the Sheriff, Under-Sheriff, and Swordbearer made a tour in the Proclamation Coach, fitted on a brake drawn by two horses.

About 2,000 people in Old Market Street gave the civic dignitaries a cheer as they drew up nearly opposite the Empire Theatre. The Lord Mayor made his speech amid further cheering.

Crowds blocked all approaches to the City Centre and the route to College Green was lined six to ten deep with cheering throngs.

Church bells sending their joyous peals across the city streets this morning set the keynote – of thanksgiving and rejoicing – for VE Day.

Churches were open from an early hour for private prayer, and during the morning good congregations assembled at many of them.

Bells pealed for an hour at St. Mary Redcliffe before the first of the thanksgiving services there. The church was filled. Among the congregation were some Allied Servicemen and a party of land girls.

Canon S. E. Swann, the vicar, read the Bishop of Bristol's message.

Shops were open everywhere and there were many queues – lengthy ones outside food stores – but the longest of all waiting to buy flags and decorations.

In streets where more and more emblems were still being placed in position, arrangements went forward for victory teas tonight for the kiddies, for open-air dancing to piano music, and for dozens of bonfires.

Children in Bedminster, like many others elsewhere in the city, made an effigy of Hitler and built a big bonfire on which to destroy it.

Ships in the harbour were fully dressed with flags, while even buses bore some signs of festivity, as for instance the vehicle which arrived from the country with wild flowers covering its bonnet.

Before the Bristol Royal Infirmary flag could be hoisted this morning, someone contrived to fly the Nazi swastika ensign at half mast over the infirmary.

The full street lighting at the Centre, Queen Square and some other surrounding streets will be on tonight, and some buildings will be floodlit.

Bedminster seemed to set the pace for celebrations, and although many other districts probably equalled their achievements in the end, nowhere can have excelled them. Ere the evening was out, every Bedminster street had to be entered beneath many arches of flags of all the Allied nations, and all the time residents continued to bring out more decorations to add to the grand array.

In other parts of the city it was largely the same story, if to a lesser degree.

1948: ZOO DEATH

Alfred the gorilla was Bristol Zoo's most popular resident. He was an orphan from the African Congo and was often seen walking around the zoo grounds wearing his trademark cardigan accompanied by a keeper. Alfred was so popular that people from all over the world sent him birthday cards every September. When his death was announced by zoo officials it was not only reported in the local press but also in the national papers. Alfred is now embalmed in Bristol Museum, and a bust of him stands outside the zoo's Ape House.

Western Daily Press, Wednesday 10 March 1948

BRISTOL WILL MISS HIM

Alfred is dead. Bristol Zoo's world-famous gorilla died in his cage at 10.00 a.m. yesterday.

Alfred, who has always disliked aeroplanes, was in his outer enclosure when a low-flying aeroplane frightened him. He ran into the inner-house where he collapsed and died five minutes later.

Alfred, who was 19 years old last September, had been less active of late.

He weighed approximately 33-stone at his prime but was only 18 stone 8 lbs at the time of his death.

Alfred, who has lived in captivity longer than any other gorilla, arrived in England from Rotterdam when he was two years of age and weighed only 27 lbs.

An expert will be coming to Bristol from London today to skin Alfred and take his measurements. He will be examined by the University of Bristol anatomy department, mounted in London and passed to Bristol Museum.

1948: THE GOOD QUADS

Bridget, Frances, Elizabeth and Jennifer Good made worldwide medical history when they were born at Bristol's Southmead Hospital. They were the world's first quadruplets to survive a Caesarean birth, but their mother was only expecting twins. The four girls, whose birth was announced on the BBC's Home Service (now Radio 4), quickly became known as the Good Quads. Their parents were bombarded with offers of food and clothing by companies keen to get their name and products some favourable publicity. The girls fronted a number of campaigns including one for Cow and Gate baby foods and another for Clark's shoes.

Western Daily Press, Monday 14 June 1948

BRISTOL'S FIRST QUADS 'DOING NICELY'

Quadruplets – all girls – were born at Southmead Hospital at 3.20 p.m. on Saturday. Last night the mother, 28-year-old Mrs Margaret Elizabeth Good of Henfield Farm, Coalpit Heath, was reported to be 'going along quite nicely'.

The babies were not due to be born until the middle of July.

'Delighted by the whole business' was Mr. Good's comment yesterday.

It was only on Friday that an x-ray examination showed Mrs Good to be the mother of quadruplets instead of the twins she was expecting.

As arrangements were made for a Caesarean operation, Mr. and Mrs Good discussed names, and as sex could not be determined chose four names of each sex.

Dr. P. Philips, medical supervisor, described to the *Western Daily Press,* the excitement among the nursing staff when it was known that quads were expected.

'We thought it better to operate' Dr. Percival Philips said. 'The mother is a strong, healthy woman, but we thought that unless we took immediate steps to deliver the babies we might lose them'.

The operation, watched by most of the maternity staff, lasted only three quarters of an hour, and the babies were born between 2 40 p.m. and 3 20 p.m.

They were immediately placed in oxygen chambers in the premature baby unit and special nursing staff of six staff nurses, a part-time nurse, and an orderly were detailed to look after them under the supervision of Sister Radcliffe.

Hourly feeds of water are fed to the babies with a pipette. Later they will be given breast milk from Mrs Good herself and from other mothers at the hospital.

The babies in the order they were born, weighed: Bridget - three pounds thirteen ounces; Frances - four pounds and a quarter of an ounce; Elizabeth – four pounds eight and a quarter ounces; Jennifer – three pounds and fourteen ounces.

All are perfectly developed above the average weight for the premature baby and are said by hospital staff to 'have a sporting chance of survival'.

Dr. Phillips said: 'So far as is known these are the first quads born in Bristol'.

'Jennifer is a little delicate, but I have every hope that we shall be able to save all of them.'

'We were so anxious that the news should not get around on Friday when the x-ray was taken. We even lost the x-ray negative for a few hours.'

Yesterday Mr. Good visited his wife in a single ward at the hospital, and then went to Keynsham to take the latest news to his wife's parents.

Mr. Good said: 'The chief worry now is getting someone to help my wife when she comes back to the farm. It is rather primitive there. We only have oil for heating and lighting, and have to fetch hot water from the dairy'.

'If we find we can't just manage I shall have to look for another place, but we hope to make good of it'.

1949: LIFT-OFF FOR THE BIG 'BRAB'

Many thousands of Bristolians worked on the Brabazon, at the time the world's biggest aircraft. It was built by the Bristol Aircraft Co. at Filton and designed to carry 100 passengers in luxury from London to New York non-stop. The 'Brab' was 50 feet high, 1,777 feet long with a wingspan of 230 feet wide. It was so big that Filton's neighbouring village of Charlton, home to some thirty families, an infant school, village hall, farmhouses and a pub was demolished to make way for a lengthened runway to

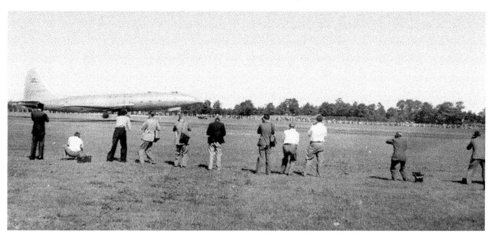

Press photographers capture the Brabazon aircraft before its maiden flight from Filton Airfield. (Courtesy of Paul Townsend under Creative Commons 2.0)

be built. Development of the Brabazon cost £12 million, but unfortunately not one commercial airline placed an order for the aircraft. Four years after its maiden flight the government announced that the Brabazon would be scrapped.

Western Daily Press, Monday 6 September 1949

LOCAL PRIDE SOARS WITH BRABAZON
Serene maiden flight earns world salute

Bristol's Brabazon surprised the world yesterday. It sailed serenely off on its maiden flight, only eight minutes after taxiing onto the main runway and a mere 24 hours after its taxiing trials commenced on Saturday morning.

So began at three minutes after noon, a new epoch in the history of British Aviation. The 130 ton Brabazon 1, with its eight 'Bristol' 'Centaurus' engines driving its four pairs of contra-rotating propellers, as the largest civil plane in the world, was about to lift off for the first time.

Twenty thousand people at vantage points around the vast airfield at Filton cheered when the silver giant, graceful and gleaming in the sunlight lifted smoothly into the air.

It circled north of Filton before making a perfect landing in less than 600 yards of the three thousand yards runway.

With Bristol Aircraft Company's Chief Test Pilot, Mr. A. J. 'Bill' Pegg, at the controls, the Brabazon, with a minimum of pre-flight fuss and a brief engine run-up at the east end of the concrete 'strip' took off in less than 500 yards, climbed steadily to 3,500 feet and flew in a 74-mile circuit in 25 minutes. Its average cruising speed was given as 140 knots - approximately 173 miles per hour,

The pilot added a human touch to this story by flying over his home at Thornbury.

For its maiden flight the Brabazon approached the west end of the runway with engines throttled and made a perfect landing, coming to a halt in less than 600 yards.

Lord Brabazon of Tara, after whom the machine is named, and Sir William Verdon Smith (Chairman of Bristol Aircraft Company) were the first to congratulate the crew as they stepped on to the tarmac.

A spokesman for the aircraft company, said: 'From now on the Brabazon will go on to normal routine testing works'.

Mr. A. Russell, Chief Designer, said: 'Our work will start in a very few weeks' time to extend the trials to higher speeds, distances and altitudes'.

1951: MAJOR OIL DISASTER

The biggest peacetime oil fire in Britain broke out on an 850-acre oil-tank farm at Avonmouth Docks in 1951. The blaze was so big that firemen from every county in the South West were called in along with their colleagues from London to tackle it. Even sailors were drafted into help. The smoke was visible as far as 100 miles away. Two men working on the oil-tank farm lost their lives in the inferno.

Western Daily Press, Friday 7 September 1951

BRISTOL FIGHT TO HOLD BIGGEST OIL FIRE
Danger of spread to adjacent compound very great
Two men reported to be missing
Cause of the blaze not yet known

Early today firemen were still fighting to stop the spread of the 14,000,000 gallon petrol and oil fire at the Regent Oil Company's compound at the Royal Edward Dock, Avonmouth. It was thought that the blaze was nearly under control and with available firefighting units it would be possible to isolate it. But there was still however a great danger of it spreading to the adjacent Cleveland Oil Company's compound and firemen sprayed the nearest Cleveland tank – empty but full of vapour – as a precaution. The wind was fanning the flames towards a string of tanks which contain one million gallons of high octane spirit.

It was officially announced that 15 large tanks and several small ones were involved. Late last night Mr. S. Ascough, Regent Oil Company's Divisional Manager said: 'I estimate 14 million gallons have gone up. The conflagration is racing down the side of the river. Truck loads of earth and sand have been brought in to reinforce the retaining wall'.

Two men were officially reported missing. They were working on the tanks when the first explosion occurred. They are Ray Hyett of Lawrence Weston and Arthur Bagg of Avonmouth.

The cause of the blaze is not yet known.

Just before midnight the General Manager of Regent Oil Company, Mr. R. Ball, arrived at the docks from London with the Chief Engineer Mr. J. Frost, and the manager of Bulk Storage Installation, Mr. M. Brown. They were met by the Western Branch Manager, Mr. F. Laine.

Early this morning a spokesman for Regent Oil said the amount of spirit involved represents less than one quarter of the company's storage at Avonmouth. 'So that although it is a catastrophic loss of spirit and storage space it is not expected that serious, or more than temporary dislocation of distribution services will result'.

It is thought by experienced firefighting officers that it is unlikely that the fire will be out before the weekend.

The fire started in a big diesel oil storage tank 50 yards from the Regent Oil Company's office block.

It was described by Mr. Ascough. 'I was by the telephone when it started. I heard an explosion and looked up and saw the No. 2 tank blow up. I sent my staff to the fire stations and called the fire brigade.

I think it is the biggest peace-time oil fire in the country'.

One of his clerks said: 'There was a flash and a big bang. Then flames roared to a terrific height. The next tank went up soon afterwards and the fire spread rapidly down the line of tanks.'

When the call was received in Bristol the firemen were lined up for their annual inspection by Her Majesty's Inspector of Fire Brigades and the Lord Mayor of Bristol.

The alarm bell rang and crews drove the eight mile journey to Avonmouth where they found four tanks in the compound blazing furiously.

1954: BRISTOL BRITANNIA CRASHES

The world's first long-haul prop-jet airliner, the Bristol Britannia, was designed and built by the Bristol Aircraft Co. at Filton. It became known as 'The Whispering Giant' on account of its quiet exterior noise and smooth flying. Only eighty-five Britannia aircraft were built before production ended in 1960. The aircraft had an undistinguished development period including two crashes, both not far from the factory where it was built. In one of the crashes fifteen people lost their lives.

Bristol Evening Post, Thursday 4 February 1954

FIGHT AGAINST TIDE TO RESCUE BRITANNIA
Giant B A C airliner in forced landing on Severn mudflats
The crew is saved

Emergency measures were pressed forward this afternoon in a bid to salvage from the mud of the Severn Estuary the second prototype Britannia airliner, which crash landed shortly before noon on Littleton Flats, about two miles north of Aust Ferry.

Technicians who had been rushed to the scene from the Bristol Aircraft Company at nearby Filton, had five to six hours in which to work before the incoming tide would reach the plane. High water at 8. 20 p.m. would engulf her.

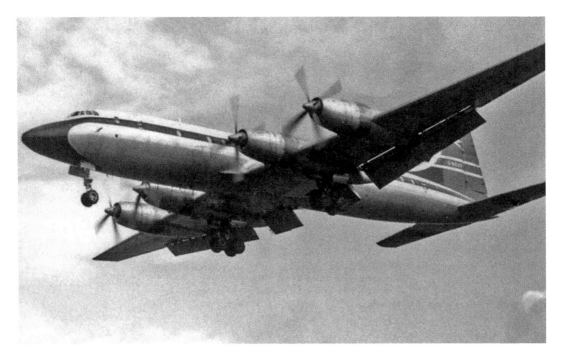

The Bristol Britannia was one of the many aircraft built by the Bristol Aeroplane Co. (Courtesy of RuthAS under Creative Commons 3.0)

The Britannia on a routine flight, was crash-landed by the Bristol Aircraft Company's Chief Test Pilot, Mr. A.J. 'Bill' Pegg with one of the engines on fire after he had searched the area in the hope of finding a suitable landing strip.

One fuel tank exploded as the plane came down, but the resulting fire was quickly extinguished and the fire appliances that were sent to the scene from a wide area including Bristol, were needed only for standby purposes.

The machine which came down on hard mud became firmly embedded in it by the force of the impact, and was extensively damaged.

Mr. Pegg and nine others in the crew, including B A C technicians and observers, as well as a co-pilot and flight engineers, clambered out unhurt.

About 20 men were quickly on the spot making arrangements for salvaging the Britannia. This is the period of spring tides.

A spokesman for the Bristol Aircraft Company said: 'We shall do everything humanly possible to salvage the plane and if we haven't the necessary equipment we shall get it'.

As soon as the damage and state of the plane were known, equipment was rushed to the scene.

Mr. G. Williams, Managing Director of the Aust Ferry, said: 'I can see the Britannia through field glasses.

From where she is lying it would appear to be a fairly easy salvage job with trailers being used from the river bank'.

He said one of his clerks heard the aircraft circling overhead. The next thing they saw, she was on the mud and a cloud of smoke rose into the air.

A senior official from the Bristol Aircraft Company, who was at the scene within half an hour of the plane coming down, told the *Evening Post* that arrangements were being made to bring a tug and barge from Avonmouth to Littleton so as to secure the aircraft before the high tide.

He said: 'We are also getting a pantechnicon from Bristol and hope to haul it over the frozen fields to a point where we can attach a hawser to the plane and secure it from the landward side.'

1955: HOW BRISTOL'S AIRPORT TOOK OFF

Bristol was always proud of its original airport, which was opened at Whitchurch, 3 miles south of the city, in 1930. It was only the third municipal airport in the country and one of the few that remained operational during the Second World War. As passenger numbers grew civic officials were looking for a much bigger site. They eventually agreed with the government on a price of £55,000 for a disused RAF station at Lulsgate Bottom, 7 miles south of Bristol. The new airport was opened in May 1957 by the Duchess of Kent. Bristol City Council ran it until 1997 when a majority shareholding was sold to a private transport operator. Bristol Airport – ever expanding – is currently handling 7 million passengers a year.

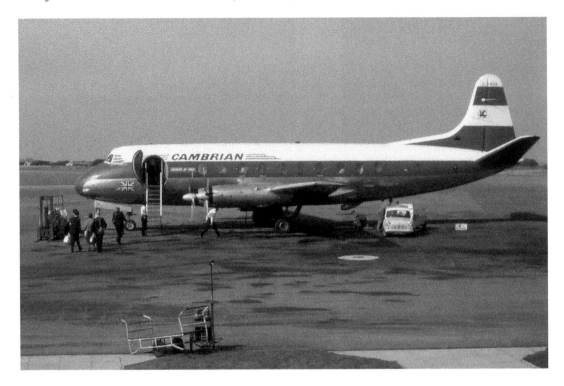

Viscounts flown by Cambrian Airways were a familiar visitor at Bristol Airport. This one is pictured in 1963. Cambrian was incorporated with British Airways in 1974. Courtesy of Arpingstone under Creative Commons 3.0)

Bristol Evening Post, Wednesday 22 June 1955

LULSGATE IS CHOSEN AS BRISTOL AIRPORT

Bristol is to have Lulsgate - a derelict war-time RAF station - as its new municipal aerodrome. The move from Whitchurch Airport will be given top priority and Lulsgate should be in full operation within a year.

The decision - the result of nearly 10 years of negotiations between the city and successive Ministers of Transport and Civil Aviation - reached Bristol in a letter from the present minister Mr. John Boyd Carpenter to the Lord Mayor Alderman Harry Crook.

It offered Lulsgate to Bristol Corporation on sale or lease.

Airport Committee Chairman, Alderman V. J. Ross said today: 'I am delighted at the news. Personally, I am in favour of buying though it will depend very largely on how much they want for it.

We shall have to spend a lot of money on the airport – for administration buildings and so on – and it is better to spend on our own property'.

Alderman Ross, who has led deputation after deputation to try and make Bristol a national airport for the West Country, said: 'Now the minister has said you can do it' – and we will do it for the citizens of Bristol are behind us.

'I am still hoping we may get some measure of financial assistance from the ministry. But even without it, it's up to Bristol to back it. We must have an airport'.

Civic officials are to 'take all immediate steps' to start negotiations with the Ministry about details of the take – over'.

As soon as plans are made, the future of Whitchurch – requisitioned by the Government since 1939 – can be foreseen as well.

The volume of air traffic from Whitchurch has grown steadily since the war. But hemmed in by housing estates and hills, with a 1,025 yard runway that cannot be lengthened, the airport has become more and more inadequate.

Lulsgate, on a plateau on the Mendip edge has open approaches for miles around. It already has one 1,300 yard and two 1,100 yard runways. Extensions to give even the biggest airliners a safety margin would probably be made.

1956: THE QUEEN OPENS NEW COUNCIL HOUSE

For 125 years a small Georgian building on Corn Street served the needs of the staff of the city council as their administrative headquarters. However, by the 1930s, with the growth of Bristol in both population and geographical size meant a much larger

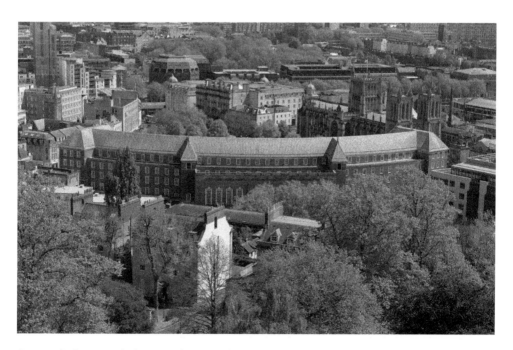

An aerial photograph showing the rear of City Hall. It was known as the Council House until 2016. (Courtesy of Rodw under Creative Commons 3.0).

building was needed. The foundation station of the new crescent-shaped Council House on College Green was laid in 1938 but building work was held up by the Second World War. It wasn't until 1956 that the new Council House was officially opened by the Queen. This was Her Majesty's first visit to the city since she was crowned three years earlier.

Bristol Evening Post, Tuesday 17 April 1956

'BRISTOL ALWAYS LINKED WITH THRONE'

To have travelled by water was the most appropriate way for her to have come to Bristol because the Avon and the city had been linked together throughout Bristol's history, the Queen told the gathering of over 500 people at the opening ceremony of the Council House.

Replying to the Loyal Address read by the Recorder, Mr. G. D. Roberts QC, the Queen said: 'My Lord Mayor, I thank you for the Loyal Address of the Aldermen and Burgesses of the City and County of Bristol.

I have been very moved by the warmth of the welcome which you and the citizens have given to me and my husband, and I am delighted to be with you today and so continue that association between the Throne and Bristol which has existed for so long.

My husband and I have been very happy to come to the very heart of Bristol by water.

It is, I think, the most appropriate way for me to come amongst you because the Avon has been linked with Bristol throughout your history.

For centuries men of Bristol have sailed down the river to voyages of discovery and in the pursuit of trade upon which your fortunes have been founded'.

Bristol, Her Majesty continued, had flourished by the enterprise of merchants and the skill and craftsmanship displayed through the materials they had brought back.

'Today, I am opening a new Council House to replace the old house which has served your needs for 125 years. The growth of your responsibility for the health and happiness of your citizens made the old house inadequate.

Here in this new Council House, you will I am sure, be able to continue to discharge with ever-increasing efficiency and success the heavy responsibility which you, My Lord Mayor, Aldermen and Councillors, carry for the well-being of the burgesses of this historic town.'

Her Majesty concluded: 'I am glad to see that in this fine building the traditions of the fine craftsmanship for which you in the West Country are acclaimed are so worthily applied.

I congratulate you on the building and all those who took part in its planning and construction. I now declare it open and I pray that success will crown the work which is undertaken here.'

Then at 12.06 p.m. the Queen drew back the oyster-coloured satin curtain which had covered the special commemoration tablet placed on the wall which separates the assembly hall and the council chamber.

Under an oak pelmet on which are five rosettes, in gilt and natural colour of the flower of Bristol, an inscription read:

'Her Majesty Queen Elizabeth 11, accompanied by His Royal Highness, The Duke of Edinburgh, honoured the City and County of Bristol on the 17th April 1956 by opening this building.'

There followed the names of Harry Crook, Lord Mayor, Alexander Pickard, Town Clerk and E. Vincent Harris, Architect.

The Dean of Bristol, the Very Rev. F. Lunt then asked the Bishop of Bristol, Dr. F.A. Cockin, to dedicate the building.

Then came one of the charming highlights of the Queen's visit when the Town Clerk, Mr. Alexander Pickard, handed to the Lord Mayor the brooch of diamonds and rubies in the shape of the flower of Bristol.

This was presented by the city to the Queen as a memento of her visit instead of the usual jewelled casket which normally accompanies the Loyal Address of Welcome.

The Lord Mayor presented the brooch to the Queen and said: 'May I thank you for graciously honouring us by opening this building and may I ask you to accept on behalf of the City and County of Bristol this memento of your visit'.

As Her Majesty examined it the Duke, who was sitting on her left looked obviously delighted with it, and leaned over from his chair to make a closer examination.

Then at 12.10 p.m. preceded by the City Sword Bearer, Mr. Jack Sealy, the Queen and the rest of the party left the dais for a brief inspection of the new council chamber.

For more than an hour before the arrival at the Council House of the Royal visitors there was an air of expectant excitement in the main entrance hall and in the assembly hall as members of the council, Bristol MPs, former Sheriffs of the city, their ladies, and the many distinguished guests chatted among themselves.

Then as they took their seats in the hall they admired the beautiful floral displays arranged on the dais upon which the Queen and the party were to sit.

Among the profusion of blooms were hydrangea, cinneraria, sysynthias and exotic plants and ferns.

Discreetly hidden among the flowers, which were predominantly mauve, blue, red and pink, were two of the four microphones used to relay the speeches.

On one side of the hall a loudspeaker relayed a military band playing such modern favourites as 'Davy Crockett' and 'Love and Marriage' before the BBC commentary of the Queen's progress up the Floating Harbour by Alan Gibson was switched on.

The tremendous cheers of the crowd, the ships' sirens and the noise of the jet aircraft flying overhead were heard and the audience burst out laughing when Mr. Gibson referred to Bristol's 'famous unicorns'.

The ceremony in the Council House Conference Hall was simple but impressive. The Royal couple sat in the high white stone room on a dais surrounded by flowers and with the mace-bearers behind.

Prompt at 12 noon the city trumpeters blew their call and the Queen and the Duke entered behind the City Sword.

Immediately the Queen gave the now standing gathering a radiant smile. She took the high chair with the Lord Mayor and Duke of Edinburgh on either side of her. The Royal couple, while they listened to the welcome read by Mr. G. D. Roberts were looking around the room and the Duke seemed particularly interested in the ceiling mural.

He glanced, too, at the bevy of photographers and film cameramen who were on a raised platform to one side of the hall.

The menu for the luncheon at the Mansion House attended by the Royal couple was simple, consisting of melon, roast duckling, green peas and new potatoes; fresh pineapple, lemon soufflé and cream and cheese and biscuits.

The wines served with the luncheon were a sherry, Reina Victoria, a hock, Deidesheimer Kieselberg Riesling Auslese, 1949, a claret, Chateau Lafite 1934, a white wine, Chateau d'Yuem 1949, and a magnum of Bristol cream and cognac.

1956: A RIGHT ROYAL WELCOME FOR THE QUEEN

Apart from opening the Council House the Queen had a number of engagements in Bristol and north Somerset where she opened Bristol Waterworks Chew Valley Lake. Along the royal route it seemed that every fraction of window and roof space was occupied and even scaffolding on building sites along the route were taken up as viewing stands – this was long before health and safety rules and regulations were part of everyday life. Dozens of school parties from across the city also packed the pavements.

Bristol Evening Post, Tuesday 17 April 1956

BRISTOL'S ROYAL DAY
Crowds follow the Queen

The Queen said this afternoon she was deeply moved by Bristol's welcome. And so enthusiastic were the Bristolians that many having had an ideal view of the Queen and Duke of Edinburgh during the morning engagements, this afternoon took up positions on the route to Chew Valley for a second sight of the royal couple.

Right to the city boundary, roads were packed with happy-noisy crowds. The weather was in keeping with the royal occasion, the sun smiled down merrily on the exhilarating scene.

The Queen emphasised how 'very moved' she was by the city's welcome when she declared open the new Council House, one of the main events of her tour of Bristol and Somerset.

Many hundreds of people started early this morning taking up vantage points, and by the time the Queen and Duke, in an open car, drove through the streets the crowds have swollen to mammoth proportions.

Somerset was the scene of the royal visit this afternoon and again vast crowds were gathering to witness Her Majesty open Bristol Water Works Chew Valley Lake which cost nearly £2 million.

Afterwards they were driving to the village of Newton St. Loe to have tea with the tenants of Duchy of Cornwall property. Later the Queen and the Duke were going to Bath Guildhall where presentations were being made to them.

At the end of the official tour the royal couple were driving to Badminton House, where they will be guests of the Duke and Duchess of Beaufort for the three-day Badminton Horse Trials.

One of the most amazing scenes in Bristol was around St. Mary Redcliffe church where police estimated 20,000 people had gathered. The royal couple were given a private 15-minute tour of the church by the vicar the Rev. Richard Cartwright. The Queen exclaimed to the Rev. Cartwright 'this wonderful church' as she was guided around it.

The Queen inspected the charter granted by Queen Elizabeth I to the Vestry of St. Mary Redcliffe giving it the right to hold a free school teaching literature and grammar.

A last-minute change in plans gave crowds waiting outside Albion Dockyard, Bristol, an unexpected glimpse of the royal party.

It had been planned that the fleet of four cars should swing into the dockyard before the Queen and the Duke alighted. Because of possible congestion, this idea was shelved.

The royal car stopped outside the gates and the Queen and the Duke passed within a few yards of the cheering crowds which surged forward through the police cordon as the Queen shook hands with Mr. Charles Hill, company chairman.

The Queen was conducted around the exhibition by Mr. Hill, and the Duke by Mr. John Hill.

A highlight of the day was a trip made by the Queen and the Duke of Edinburgh by barge to Broad Quay, part of Bristol Docks. They passed within a few yards of the spot where a water pageant was staged for the entertainment of Queen Elizabeth I on her visit to Bristol in 1574.

Punctual to the minute, a formation of 12 Vampire jet fighters of the 501 County of Gloucester Squadron of the R. Aux. A.F. screamed over the City Centre as the royal barge carrying the Queen and the Duke of Edinburgh, sailed through the City Docks to the landing stage at Broad Quay.

Flowers and cheers greeted the radiant Queen and the smiling Duke of Edinburgh as they stepped from the royal train at Temple Meads station at 10 o'clock this morning to be greeted by the Duke of Beaufort, who introduced civic dignitaries and other distinguished personages.

Four anti-aircraft guns on The Downs boomed their salute as the royal train drew into the station...and all Bristol knew the Queen had arrived.

1956: FLOWER OF BRISTOL

There can't be many cities that have a floral emblem as a symbol. But Bristol has its Flower of Bristowe - an ancient spelling of the city's name. It grows wild in parts of the Avon Gorge to a height of between 2 and 3 feet and each summer it produces small five-petalled red florets shaped like a cross. The shape of the flower was used in the making of a jewelled brooch given to the Queen when she opened the Council House.

Western Daily Press, Wednesday 18 April 1956

'FLOWER OF BRISTOL' DELIGHTED QUEEN
City's gift replaced diamond clasp on her coat

The Queen arrived with the Duke of Edinburgh in Bristol yesterday morning wearing a diamond clasp pinned to the left shoulder of her coat. When she left, the city's gift of a jewelled brooch in the form of the 'Flower of Bristol' had taken its place.

Within 20 minutes of receiving the gift with obvious delight from the Lord Mayor (Alderman Harry Crook) in the Conference Hall of the Council House, the Queen had put it on. As soon as she got into the Mansion House for lunch she pinned the three-inch long brooch, which is in rubies and diamonds, to her dress. And after lunch she removed the diamond clasp she had worn on her coat all the morning and put the 'Flower of Bristol' in its place for the rest of the day.

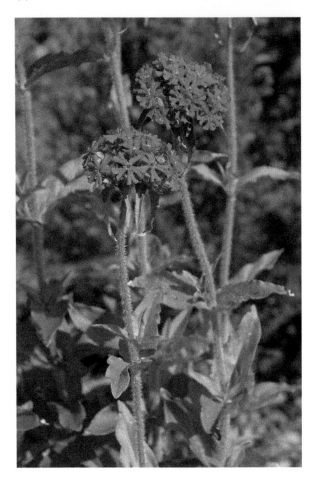

The flower of Bristol, known to botanists as Lychnis Chalcedonica, grows to a height of around 2 feet. (Courtesy of Wouter Hagens under Creative Commons 3.0)

This seemed to typify that happy spirit in which the Queen and Duke spent their time in Bristol and Somerset.

Yesterday was a stop-watch day for them. Although the Queen came principally to open Bristol's Council House at College Green and to inaugurate Bristol Waterworks Chew Valley Lake, the royal programme took in a great deal more.

Everywhere a tumultuous reception awaited the Queen and the Duke. At places in Bristol the thousands who turned out to see them stood six deep, and one was left to marvel at how few people were apparently required to keep the life of Bristol going.

The largest crowd the Queen and Duke were presented with all day was on College Green, outside the Council House. The view from behind the Queen as she acknowledged the cheers from the balcony was reminiscent of the solid masses of people in the Victory celebrations.

Villages along the route through Somerset all had their dense knots of sightseers, but many sparse stretches in between allowed the Royal procession to pick up lost time at speeds of up to 60 miles per hour.

The first hint of the Queen's arrival in Bristol came at four minutes to 10 with a whispered message among the detectives standing on platform nine at Temple Meads – 'She's passing the East Box'.

The row of people standing on the 10-yards wide strip of red carpet on the platform, waiting to be presented to the Queen made the last tugs at hats, coats and uniforms; the 'Hartlebury Castle' slid into the station pulling the royal train ... and the day had begun.

Was it an omen that the weather was not to be sunshine all the way that the first person off the train was a member of the household staff bearing two umbrellas and a fur cape?

And when the welcomes were over and the Queen walked from the station, she was presented with a scene which was to be repeated many times. Crowds many deep, crammed windows, courageous Royalists clinging to precarious roof-top spots of vantage, and endless splashes of red, white and blue (for yesterday was a great day for the flag sellers).

The face of Bristol, which the Queen and the Duke saw was a friendly, though rather painted one.

The lustiest cheers came from schoolchildren, notably at Cumberland Road and Upper Belgrave Road, and it was most noticeable that the Royal car cruised at the slowest past groups of children.

1957: BRITANNIA CRASH DEATHS

Just three years after a Bristol Britannia aircraft crash-landed on the mud flats of the Severn Estuary, another Britannia came down on the outskirts of Bristol with tragic consequences: all those on board lost their lives.

Bristol Evening Post, Wednesday 6 November 1957

BRITANNIA CRASHES AT DOWNEND: 15 DIE

The crew of 15 – many technicians – were killed when a Bristol Britannia airliner on a test flight crashed in the Overndale Road area of Downend today.

The aircraft – the first prototype of the model 301 long range series – blew up immediately on impact, hurling debris into houses, tearing huge holes in roofs and shattering walls and windows – but people in their homes escaped death.

Fire engines raced to the scene as a helicopter from the Bristol Aircraft Company flew over the scene.

The plane fell almost into the gardens of eight newly-erected houses. Ten houses were damaged.

It was a scene of indescribable confusion at the rear of the damaged houses. The largest piece of the Britannia in sight was no bigger than a small car. One of the largest pieces which seemed to be a twisted battered engine bay was between Nos. 45–47 Overndale Road. A few yards away stood a pram.

Scores of housewives and pedestrians in many parts of the city had earlier seen the plane in distress. It was 'wobbling' and 'banking steeply' before it crashed.

Within seconds a huge pillar of smoke rose, sending dozens of people to the telephone to raise the alarm.

Piloting the Britannia was the Bristol Aircraft Company's Assistant Chief Test Pilot, Hugh Statham, 47, who joined the company in 1940 and has flown well over 5,000 hours, mostly in Britannias. During the war he was engaged on production testing of Beaufort's and Beaufighter's.

Of the 15 people on board the aircraft, eight were BAC employees. Their relatives were being informed before a list of names was issued. The others on board were representatives of the Air Ministry and the De Havilland aircraft company.

At least two people living in Overndale Road were injured and taken to hospital.

1957: BRITANNIA CRASH: AIRCRAFT FIRM'S STATEMENT

Air accident investigation inquiries were started immediately after the Britannia crash. The following day the aircraft makers, the Bristol Aircraft Co., issued a statement for newspaper publication.

Bristol Evening Post, Thursday 7 November, 1957

BRITANNIA SWUNG ROUND JUST BEFORE CRASH: BAC

Seconds before the Bristol Britannia crashed at Downend yesterday it swung round in mid-air, Bristol Aircraft Company said this afternoon.

After checking dozens of statements the company announced: 'From many eye witness accounts it seems that the aircraft, after making a turn to port in a position to the south-east of the airfield at about 1,500 feet, swung away to starboard, went into a deep turn, lost height and struck the ground.

So far as anything may be stated with certainty at this stage, the aircraft was not on fire in the air.

Mr. J. Duggan, deputy chief inspector of accidents for the Ministry of Transport and Civil Aviation, and a six-man team began their investigation in Overndale Road. Technicians from BAC are co-operating with them.'

1958: ITV COMES WEST

The BBC's television monopoly of West Country viewers ended as Television Wales & West (TWW) went on air for the first time. The ITV company had specially built studios at Arnos Vale in Bristol and at Pontcanna Farm, Cardiff. The first local person to appear on TWW in a quiz specially created for the station – which was broadcast from the Grand Hotel, Broad Street – was Bert Tann, the Bristol Rovers manager. TWW lost its franchise in 1968, when it was taken away by the Independent Broadcasting Authority.

Bristol Evening Post, Tuesday 14 January 1958

THOUSANDS IN THE WEST CAN NOW GET COMMERCIAL TV

Commercial television arrives in the West today. For the first time, thousands of viewers in Bristol, Somerset and South Gloucestershire have the choice of two television programmes.

Tonight's transmissions from 4.45 to midnight are an exciting introduction to the first-class entertainment and information service now available to every suitably-equipped West home at the flick of a switch.

TWW Ltd (Television Wales and the West) says that this service will be maintained.

A glance at tonight's fare shows just how well the promises of top-quality entertainment are being fulfilled. In the show at seven o'clock 'Stars Rise in the West', Jack Hylton (whose shows are a high spot of the ITV week) introduces stars with South Wales and West connections ... people like Shirley Bassey, Stanley Baker, Petula Clark, Tommy Cooper, Donald Houston, Ronald Lewis, Tessie O'Shea, Ralph Reader, Harry Secombe, Sir Ralph Richardson, Donald Sinden and Naunton Wayne.

Then comes 'Emergency Ward 10', followed by a quiz game televised live from the TWW studios with an outside broadcast link to bring in a competitor from Bristol. 'Chelsea at Nine', a news review, and an Arthur Askey film complete the evening's viewing.

This is no first-night flash-in-the pan. It is typical of the standard of viewing which has been set elsewhere in the country and which now comes to Bristol and the West.

The pick of the ITV network programmes, plus regional contributions from the magnificent £20,000 TWW studios at Pontcanna Farm, Cardiff, will reach viewers via the St. Hilary Transmitting station – the sixth to be built by the authority.

The TWW studios, as the company's president, Lord Derby, has said 'are something of which not only we, but also South Wales and the West of England can be proud.'

'They are unique in that they have been built from the ground up and not through the modification of existing theatre or cinema premises. Every modern development has been incorporated giving TWW, the facilities for presenting its programmes in the best possible way'.

TWW is determined to live up to its president's promise: 'I firmly believe that people in South Wales and the West of England will find us a great asset to their leisure hours and will feel that we have more than lived up to the sense of responsibility which is so essential in this medium of entertainment.'

1958: POP CONCERT CHAOS

Police reinforcements were called to Colston Street as screaming fans blocked the road to traffic as their pop idol Frankie Vaughan was singing at two concerts in the Colston Hall. Vaughan, who was known as 'Mr. Moonlight' after one of his early hits, made more than eighty records during his showbiz career and attracted 'full houses' at his concerts. This was the era when pop concerts were being staged at the Colston Hall most nights of the week by a local promoter.

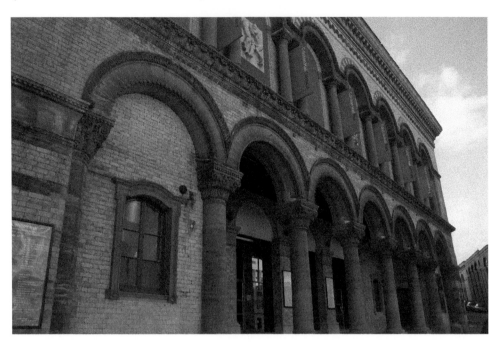

Bristol's Colston Hall. (Courtesy of Steinsky under Creative Commons 3.0)

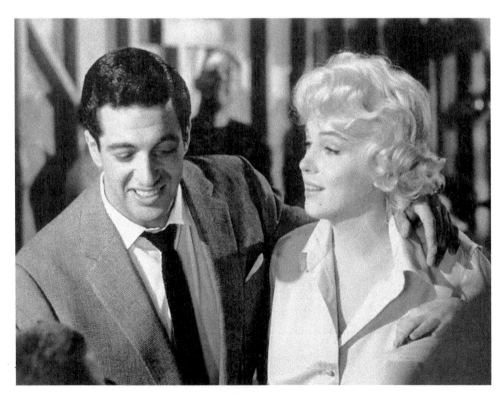

Frankie Vaughan, seen here with actress Marilyn Monroe in the 1960 film *Let's Make Love*. (Courtesy of 20th Century Fox under Creative Commons 3.0)

Bristol Evening Post, Thursday 30 April 1958

FANS BESIEGE FRANKIE VAUGHAN
Noses punched and chairs overturned in near riot.

Hundreds of screaming teenage fans besieged the fabulous 'pop' singer Frankie Vaughan on the stage of the Colston Hall, Bristol, last night. Before he could be whisked to safety, noses were punched, chairs overturned and girls trampled in a near riot.

Teenagers had rushed the stage as he started his last number.

As girls closed in, band instruments were passed to safety over the heads of the crowd. The singer and the 'mike' disappeared in a welter of loving arms and the words of 'Garden of Eden' were lost in the shrieks of the mob.

Stage attendants cleared a way off the stage apron and Frank fled to his dressing room.

It was a disappointing ending for one of the most intimate Colston Hall concerts ever given by such a famous star of stage and screen.

Hundreds of the audience hoped that the mob could be shepherded back to their seats and the concert ended in a proper manner, but there was no hope of that. The band played 'God Save The Queen' and the fans jostled out to join the hundreds already blocking Colston Street in the hope of getting a final glimpse of their idol.

Perhaps the fans shouldn't be blamed too much for there was a magic fever in the air ... the star had been given a great build-up.

Frank Weir and his orchestra gave the audience a good softening up – if any was needed. 'Swinging Shepherd Blues', 'When the Saints Come Marching In' and 'The Indian Love Call', were included in a programme that had the hand-jive going.

There was a memorable first appearance too of a 17-year-old youngster, whose name is worth remembering. David Fountain gave 'Oh Boy' and 'Jailhouse Rock' in traditional 'rock' style and then shattered the audience by singing 'Come Back to Sorrento', and with a surprisingly good voice.

But there was more to come. Murray Campbell, up-and-coming trumpeter fanned the flames a bit higher and TV star Marion Ryan brought everyone to their feet.

This dainty little Miss – in a bodice glistening with sequins – included 'Love me forever', 'I ain't gonna go' and 'Rock-a-billy wedding' in her programme and even enticed one young male onto the stage to encourage girls to join him and at one time started a rock 'n' roll session on the stage.

The fans got wilder and wilder. More and more ventured onto the stage to crouch near the exits. Each time Frankie Vaughan took a step girls flung themselves at him. At one time he wore more round his neck than the pearls in a necklace.

It was when he started to sing his closing number 'Garden of Eden' that the trouble really got under way.

Closer and closer edge the fans until finally he went down under a welter of bodies.

It was several minutes before a way could be cleared to get the star of the show off the stage. By that time his manager had been punched in the face.

They locked themselves in the dressing room and they were still there an hour after the show had ended, besieged by hundreds of shrieking girls.

Over the telephone to the *Evening Post* at midnight the star's manager said: 'This is the most fantastic reception we have ever had anywhere in this country. We are used to being mobbed – but we have never seen anything like this before'.

Members of the Frankie Vaughan Fan Club were outside the dressing room door apologising for the behaviour of other fans, and outside the Colston Hall, hundreds more wanted to get a last glimpse of the star. They even stopped cars driving up Colston Street to make sure he wasn't hiding in the back.

But Frankie, like the money he sings about was safely locked away.

1958: THIS IS BRISTOL CALLING

Bristol was chosen as the city in which to carry out a major advance in Britain's telecommunications system. When telephone engineers were happy that their backroom trials were successful, the Postmaster General invited the Queen to the Bristol Telephone Exchange to make a special call.

Bristol Evening Post, Friday 5 December 1958

THE QUEEN MAKES THE FIRST TWOPENNY CALL

The country's first twopenny trunk call was made in Bristol this afternoon by the Queen thus opening a new telephone service for 18,000 phones on the Bristol Central Exchange.

Standing on a dais at the exchange, the Queen dialled 031 CAL 3636. And 365 miles away, the Lord Provost of Edinburgh picked up the phone to receive her call.

The Queen made her call at the invitation of the Postmaster-General Mr. Ernest Marples on a streamlined, light blue telephone connected directly to Grace, the electronic robot which controls Subscriber Trunk Dialling, only a few feet behind her.

As she dialled, each numeral and letter of the Lord Provost's number flashed up on a special indicator at the back of the dais. The 150 specially invited guests in the first floor room at the exchange where Grace is housed could watch each stage as Her Majesty's call went through.

She said: 'This is the Queen speaking from Bristol. Good afternoon, Lord Provost'.

The Lord Provost replied: 'Good afternoon your Majesty. May I with humble duty offer you the loyal greetings of the City of Edinburgh.'

The Queen then said: 'Would you please convey my greetings to them. I am always interested in any development that brings my people closer together. In a few moments Bristol subscribers will be able to make trunk calls by merely dialling the right number in a radius of 300 miles. In time, the whole United Kingdom will enjoy the advantage of the new service that the Post Office has introduced.'

The Lord Provost concluded: 'May I express my gratitude to your majesty for the honour that you have done to me and to Scotland by making the first call in this service to me.'

One of the most interested spectators was the Duke of Edinburgh who had earlier accompanied the Queen on a tour of the exchange and of the Twopenny Telephone exhibition in the Equity and Law Building in Baldwin Street.

In the exhibition Mr. Marples, a lively little figure full of enthusiasm, had demonstrated to the Queen the advantage to her when, eventually Windsor Castle is connected to London by Subscriber Trunk Dialling.

Then he told the Queen she will be able to dial Buckingham Palace direct from Windsor Castle without having to enlist the aid of an operator. It will be at least 1960 before this happens.

On the special stand which has been set up to make demonstrations of Subscriber Trunk Dialling possible, he invited the Queen to make a trial call before going to the exchange for the real thing.

After the Queen had made the call, the Postmaster-General presented to her the instrument with which she had made it.

Then accompanied again by the Duke of Edinburgh and Mr. Marples she descended to the ground floor for a 15 minute tour of the switch room.

There she chatted with 100 girl telephone operators seated at the switchboard panels lining the walls of the huge room.

1961: 'FAIREST CHURCH' UNDER THREAT

When it was revealed that the stonework of St Mary Redcliffe Church was crumbling away and the building was in danger of decay its vicar, the Revd Canon Richard Cartwright, lost no time in putting his entrepreneurial skills to use. He sought – and got – permission from his church council for leave from his duties at Redcliffe so he could make a tour of America to raise funds for the repairs. On one visit to the United States he covered some 17,000 miles in five weeks preaching and giving talks about Redcliffe. Many individual Americans and various organisations made generous donations. There were gifts too, from as far away as Australia. Back in Bristol one pensioner sent in a book of postage stamps along with a few pence.

Bristol Evening Post, Friday 7 July 1961

SHOCK REPORT ON ST. MARY REDCLIFFE

For the second time in 30 years St. Mary Redcliffe – 'the fairest, goodliest and most famous parish church in England' – was how Queen Elizabeth I once described it – faces a crisis.

Much of the magnificent stonework of the tower has been found to be dangerous and seriously decayed as a result of pollution by industrial smoke and fumes.

It will cost at least £150,000 to renovate the defective stonework and medieval lead work, and two and a half years or more to complete the work.

'It has come as a great shock to us' says the vicar, the Rev. Canon Richard Cartwright who this weekend launches an international appeal for £115,000 to help pay for the renovations. The balance of the money is being met out of the church's resources. It is hoped to raise the money by the end of the year and to hold a thanksgiving service on December 31.

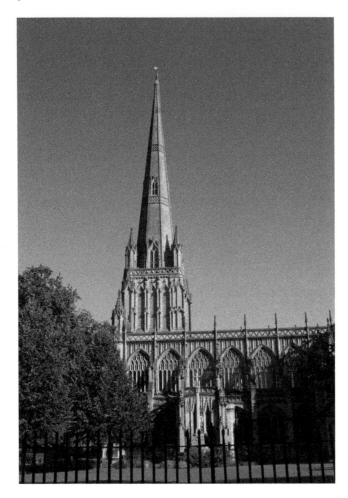

St Mary Redcliffe Church.
(Photo credit: Trevor Naylor)

'For the glory of St. Mary Redcliffe to remain this work has to be carried out and the money found' said the senior churchwarden Dr. A.M. MacLachan. 'Restoration is the object, not mending and patching'.

Among those who are associating themselves with the appeal and seeking the support of others are: The Duke of Beaufort; the Bishop of Bristol (the Rt. Rev Oliver Tomkins); the Lord Mayor of Bristol (Alderman Charles Smith); Lord Sinclair of Cleeve; Sir Reginald Verdon Smith; Sir Egbert Cadbury; Sir Foster Robinson; the Master of the Society of Merchant Venturers (Mr. W. G. Beloe); and Mr. John Betjeman.

Restoration work is being entrusted to a Bristol firm, William Cowlin and sons, who have already started operations.

It is the third major renovation in just over a century.

From time to time small pieces of stone, believed to have been affected by frost, fell from the church but the gravity of the situation was not fully appreciated until last October when a large section of stonework was found smashed on a pavement on Redcliffe Hill, alongside the church.

Immediate steps were taken to close the pathway to the public and for an expert examination of the whole façade to be carried out.

The tower was encased in scaffolding and to enable a thorough investigation to be made, and to ensure the most careful recording of the intricate details of the medieval stonework, more than 5,000 photographs embracing all the stone have been taken.

Canon Cartwright and the church authorities are confident that there are many people throughout the country and abroad who will want to support the appeal to mark the fact that for close on 800 years the church's beauty has 'witnessed to the eternal truth and goodness of God and helped many to worship him'.

1962: A WHITE WINTER

Boxing Day 1962 saw the start of one of the most extreme winters the country had seen for many years. Bristolians woke to find several inches of snow had fallen overnight. There were a further thirty-seven snow falls up to the beginning of March 1963 when a thaw set in.

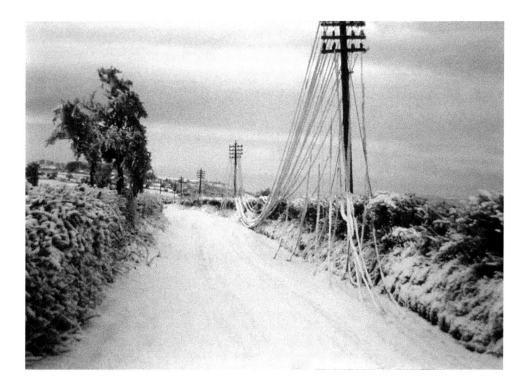

Snowdrifts in the winter of 1962/63 closed many roads in and around Bristol. (Courtesy of Howard Dublin under Creative Commons 3.0)

Bristol Evening Post, Friday 28 December 1962

BRISTOL GETS NEW FREEZE-UP WARNING

Another big freeze-up will hit Bristol tonight.

The weather office at Filton warned of approaching snow and a hard frost which could paralyse road traffic.

At 3.40 p.m. today the Fahrenheit reading was down to 24.1 degrees and falling steadily. Snow was reported coming north from Devon on the south coast.

By later afternoon it was already the coldest in Bristol since Boxing Day morning.

The AA warned: 'A hard frost can make slushy roads into ice rinks. If you needn't drive, stay home.'

Many Bristol motorists and cyclists came to work by bus today. The manager of a city centre multi-storey car park said: 'I reckon 20% of our regulars are missing.'

City buses were full. A spokesman for Bristol Omnibus Company said: 'City services are running normally. Though we are still having a bit of trouble in the Weston direction, and we can't get to Dundry. We are expecting a heavy homeward rush hour.'

Those who came by car faced a long crawl to work – and can expect the same in reverse tonight.

One motorist took three hours to reach his Bristol offices from Shipham – normally a half an hour's drive away. Another took half an hour over a half mile journey through Long Ashton, where the Weston road saw spectacular jams reaching from Bristol to Flax Bourton, a distance of seven miles.

1962: ROAD CHAOS

For several months roads were blocked, public transport was unable to run properly and many villages around Bristol were cut off. There were no frost-free nights for two months.

Bristol Evening Post, Monday 31 December 1962

IT'S MISERY MONDAY
New road chaos as West waits for thaw

It was misery Monday for Bristol and the whole of the South West today.

And despite forecasters' promises of a slow thaw, the icy grip of the worst blizzard since 1947 reduced west road conditions to chaos and confusion.

The only bright spots were central areas of Bristol and other large towns. Armies of workmen shovelled streets clear to get town buses back to normal.

In Bristol today it took 1,000 men to keep the roads clear. They shovelled tens of thousands of tons of snow into lorries for tipping into the river.

Tons of salt and grit were spread on icy roads.

Mr. H. Ellis, the City Transport and Cleansing Officer, said 150 miles of Bristol bus routes had been ploughed and gritted.

But Bristol Omnibus Company were unable to get through to several country districts. There were no buses to Portishead at mid-day.

On the Bristol–Gloucester route only half of the distance could be covered. Buses ran from Gloucester to Dursley, and in the opposite direction, from Bristol to Winterbourne. The middle stretch was quite impassable.

Tog Hill was 'hopeless' said a bus company spokesman. Buses to Chippenham were terminating at Wick.

In Bristol, city services were running, although to an erratic timetable. On the railway, West Region were running two hourly services between Bristol and Paddington, but services to South Wales, the Midlands and the North were almost normal.

1963: THE FIRST LADY

Although Bristol has had mayors since 1216 and Lord Mayors since 1899, a woman had never held the office of First Citizen until the second half of the twentieth century. Councillor Florence Brown made civic history when her fellow councillors elected her Lord Mayor in 1963. Mrs Brown, who had been a councillor for nearly thirty years, had served on many of the council's committees, including those that looked after the interests of children and education.

Western Daily Press, Wednesday 21 May 1963

THE FIRST WOMAN LORD MAYOR OF BRISTOL

Alderman Mrs Florence Brown, who was born within a stone's throw of Bristol Council House, yesterday became the city's first woman Lord Mayor.

Wearing a black velvet dress, she received the symbols of office – the gold mayoral chain, the civic sword and the fur Cap of Maintenance – from the retiring Lord Mayor, Alderman Leonard Stevenson.

Mrs Brown was cheered upon her election at the council's annual meeting. Later, when she presided for the first time over a routine meeting of the council she wore the rich, scarlet robes of Lord Mayor.

She told the council: 'I feel this honour is a reward for the work women have done on the council and in the city. I am happy that women's work is being recognised'.

Mrs Brown was first elected to Bristol City Council in 1937 and had been a member of the Education Committee for 27 years. She also served on the Children's Committee.

She was accompanied yesterday by her husband, Mr. Frederick Brown, who will be her consort during her term of office.

Mrs. Brown went to work for a Bristol tobacco firm as a tobacco leaf stripper at the age of 14, and acted as a trade union representative at the firm.

1963: THE BEATLES MAKE THEIR BRISTOL DEBUT

Four lads who formed a rock 'n' roll band in Liverpool in 1960 quickly took the pop world – both in this country and overseas – by storm. The first record by the Beatles, 'Love Me Do', not only got into the British charts but also topped the American singles chart in 1962. The next year the Beatles made their Bristol debut: two appearances at the city's main music venue, the Colston Hall. In March 1963 they were a support act for American pop singers Tommy Rose and Chris Montez who were on tour. Eight months later the Beatles were back and sang ten of their own songs to a 'full house' of 2,000 fans.

Bristol Evening Post, Post Friday 15 November 1963

THEY'RE HERE

The Beatles are here. They swept into Bristol this afternoon and within 10 seconds were locked away from their screaming fans.

They stopped their Austin Princess in a Bedminster side street while their chauffeur rang to warn the Colston Hall. Then, piloted by an *Evening Post* car through dense traffic, they shot through the Centre and to safety.

Before the crowds realised that THEY were here at last, the black limousine swung across Colston Street and into the Colston Hall yard.

Girls ran forward screaming but a chain of policemen slammed the gates in their face.

The Beatles had driven non-stop from their Exeter hotel touching 70 miles an hour at times on the A38.

Now they will remain locked up until the rescue operation to get them to their secret hotel after tonight's shows.

The city was gripped with Merseymania this afternoon as Operation Beatle went into operation.

The operation itself was something out of James Bond for secrecy.

Hundreds of girls in tight jeans laden with sandwiches and flasks of coffee besieged all entrances to the Colston Hall for eight hours before The Beatles were due to appear.

'We don't mind how long we wait; they're lovely' said 15 year old Pam Harvey of Collins Street, Avonmouth.

Scores of girls never turned up at work today. They said they would rather lose their jobs than miss The Beatles.

'They make me sick in a nice kind of way' said a 16 year old in red boots.

And Sue Godfrey, 15, of King Street, Avonmouth, said: 'We'll see The Beatles even if we have to break in.'

Back-alley touts hawked tickets at rocketing black market prices, sweet shops sold out of jelly babies (the Beatle sweet) and pin-up pictures were snapped up.

By lunch-time the Colston Hall's red doors were covered with chalked up slogans like 'We Love Paul' and 'Bring Us The Beatles'.

Some fans waited 10 hours: 'We must be here for the atmosphere' they said. One girl tried to climb a 15 foot wall at the rear of the hall.

Fans swarmed into the *Evening Post* offices this afternoon after a rumour that The Beatles were touring our offices.

Regrettably, they are NOT.

And how did The Beatles prepare for their Bristol concert? This was their time-table:

2 a.m. off to bed in their Exeter Hotel after a turkey, ham and Horlicks supper.

9.30 a.m. awake, send for breakfast.

10 .00 a.m. Back in bed and fast asleep

'The boys are determined to be at their best for the Bristol fans tonight' said their manager.

Noon: Up and around.

12.30 p.m. Leave hotel un-noticed and drive off for Bristol.

They were given VIP treatment all the way to Bristol. At checkpoint Ringo on the Exeter city boundary a Devon County police car manned by plain-clothes police officers took over escort duties from the Exeter police.

At Checkpoint McCartney on the Somerset-Devon border there was another changeover.

Up the A38 The Beatle procession swept, and on Bedminster Down, Bristol police stood by to take over.

Iron Curtain secrecy surrounded one big question the fans were asking:

Where were the Beatles staying tonight?

Every big Bristol hotel denied they had rooms booked for the boys.

This afternoon it was believed that the Beatles planned to drive to a Weston-super-Mare hotel after the show.

They spent a week at Weston in August...

1964: HOTEL ETIQUETTE RULES

The guest list down the years at the Grand Hotel in Broad Street in the city centre is certainly impressive. Writer William Thackeray ate and supped ale there, as did the poet Samuel Taylor Coleridge. Samuel Plimsoll, politician and safety at sea campaigner, was also a guest. During the Second World War Prime Minister Winston Churchill booked into the hotel when he toured devastated parts of the blitzed city. In the 1960s and 1970s pop bands on tour often stayed at the Grand Hotel when they were appearing at the nearby Colston Hall. But one particular group, the Rolling Stones, who wanted to dine in the Grand's restaurant, weren't welcome.

Bristol Evening Post, Monday 11 May 1964

'TOO SCRUFY' STONES ARE REFUSED LUNCH

Pop idols The Rolling Stones were refused lunch in the restaurant of Bristol's Grand Hotel this afternoon because they looked too scruffy.

Singer Mick Jagger wandered into the restaurant wearing a grey striped sweatshirt and jeans at 1. 20 p.m. to be met by the tail-coated headwaiter Mr. Dick Court.

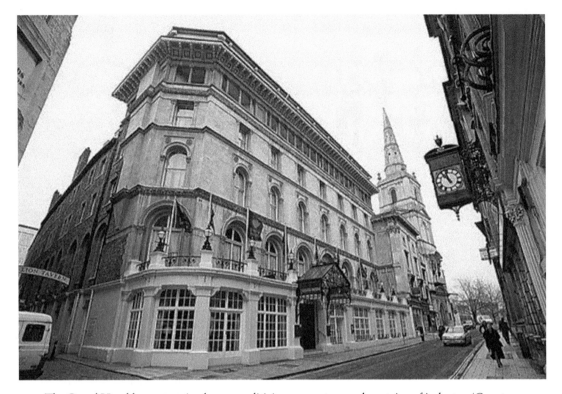

The Grand Hotel has entertained many politicians, pop stars and captains of industry. (Courtesy of Andrew Gustar under Creative Commons 2.0)

'Excuse me, Sir, but we cannot serve you unless you wear a tie and jacket. We can arrange to lend you suitable clothes if you wish to eat here' Mr. Court told him.

Jagger retired to the cocktail bar. 'I'm not going to dress up in their clothes' he said. 'We dress like this and that's that'.

Mr. Court said: 'I realise the gentleman is something of a celebrity among the young people, but that does not change the position. I would feel compelled to refuse service to anyone – even a king – if he did not dress correctly. It is a strict rule of the house'.

The Rolling Stones manager, Ian Stewart, was annoyed at the ban: 'We are guests here, and we have paid well for accommodation. Why should they refuse us food?'

Drummer Charlie Watts, wearing a tie and brown jacket said: 'I suppose they'll serve me but I'm not going in there alone'.

And the Rolling Stones trooped off in search of steaks at a nearby restaurant.

Mr. M. McFeyden, hotel manager said: 'We insist on this rule – other guests in the restaurant could be embarrassed. We accept modern vogue in dress – button-up shirts and so on – but no jeans and T-Shirts'.

The Rolling Stones eventually lunched off curried prawns at the Bali Restaurant in Park Street, Bristol.

Promoter Terry Olpin, who took them there, said: 'We created quite a sensation when we arrived. There were girls hanging out of the windows all up Park Street'.

1964: THE BEATLES ARE 'FLOUR-BOMBED'

For the last night of their UK tour towards the end of 1964, the Beatles played at the Colston Hall, this time topping the bill. It was a sellout concert with all 2,000 tickets being sold months in advance of the show. High-level security was in force in and around the hall as thousands of fans who couldn't get a ticket packed the street outside all day. But the security cordon inside the hall was broken during the concert itself in a most unusual way.

Bristol Evening Post, Wednesday 11 November 1964

THEY SAID IT WITH FLOUR

A practical joker risked his life last night to tip a bagful of flour over the Beatles from a 60 ft high ceiling of Bristol's Colston Hall.

The screaming audience went wild with delight as a great white cloud fell from the roof covering John, Paul, Ringo and George with flour.

With brilliant timing it struck from above just as the Beatles hit the last chord of their quietest number – 'If I Fell'.

The Beatles collapsed in fits of laughter pointing at each other and dancing around the stage in stitches.

There was flour in their hair, on their suits, in their eyebrows, in their guitars, and all over Ringo's drums.

Ringo turned his tom-tom upside down in a vain attempt to clear off the flour. Paul bent double with laughter, grabbed the mike and shouted: 'It's the last night of our tour, you see' – then broke into giggles again.

The audience sat just roaring and shrieking with laughter until the Beatles recovered enough to launch into Ringo's song 'I Wanna Be Your Man'.

But backstage panic reigned. The mystery joker had breached the 'foolproof' security system in the hall. Every door to the roof was locked.

And Colston Hall manager Mr. Ken Cowley sent his staff on a lightning search for the culprit. All they found was an empty flour bag lying on the plasterboard ceiling beside the hole through which the flour fell.

And all the evidence pointed to the culprit having been one of the Beatles supporting team.

A baffled Mr. Cowley said: 'So far as I can see that's the only answer. Nobody from outside could possibly have got up there. The joke itself was magnificent. The thing that worries me is that somehow our security measures were dodged.'

'And even more worrying is the fact that the joker risked his life. One false step onto part of that slender ceiling and he would have plunged 50ft to the stage possibly injuring one of the Beatles as well as himself.'

'There are four ways up to the roof. One is from the back street. That door is still secure; one is through the battery room – that door is still locked and tied. One is from the dressing rooms but the door lock is unbroken.'

'The other is from the yard through the caretaker's flat, and anyone going through there would have been seen – unless, maybe, it was an artist who went unchallenged.'

At the end of the show the Beatles raced off stage and down to their waiting car, still smothered in flour.

Tour manager Mr. John Clapson said: 'They were knocked out by the flour joke. They thought it was hilarious.'

'I suppose it could have been another of the boys on the tour who did it. But I have no idea who'.

1965: ROAD IMPROVEMENTS

Roads, homes, shops and pubs at Hotwells were bulldozed to the ground to make way for a flyover system spanning the River Avon at Cumberland Basin. The scheme took two years to build and was the first project of its kind in Bristol. It was designed to assist traffic flow by the use of roads at different levels, especially when the Plimsoll swing bridge was opened to let shipping in and out of the City Docks.

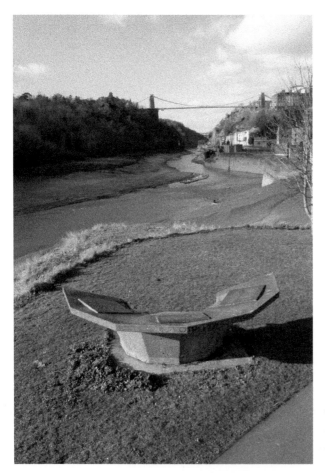

The plaques underneath Cumberland Basin Flyover that Minister of Transport unveiled. (Photo credit: Trevor Naylor)

Bristol Evening Post, Wednesday 14 April 1965

SIRENS HOOT AS FRASER PRESSES THE BUTTON

Ships sirens hooted down the Avon Gorge this afternoon as Bristol's huge Cumberland Basin roads scheme was opened.

Crowds cheered and motorists queued as Mr. Tom Fraser MP, the Minister of Transport, pressed a button to swing the bridge open to vehicles.

Then at 12 30 p.m. precisely, the first cars poured on to the concrete ramps of the £2,650,000 system.

Motorists had been queuing back onto the Weston-super-Mare road and circulating around blocks in the Hotwells area waiting for the barriers to be lifted so that they could be among the first to drive over the new swing bridge.

Despite steady rain, scores of pedestrians swarmed across the bridge, which enabled a new view to be enjoyed of the Avon Gorge.

At the opening ceremony Mr. Fraser unveiled commemorative plaques watched by the civic guests through closed circuit television. The three plaques, each one on a specially-built concrete pedestal on the bank of the River Avon, are beneath the flyover system

Every precaution has been taken to avoid a hitch. Arrangements had been made to swing the bridge by hand in case of a power failure.

But there was one short hold-up. Gates guarding the bridge failed to open as Mr. Fraser, the Lord Mayor, Cllr. Kenelm Dalby, and the chairman of the Planning Committee, Cllr. Wally Jenkins, wanted to pass through.

After a couple of minutes the all-clear was given and the official party were able to walk across the bridge to their cars for a circuit of the new scheme.

The Minister used a pair of engraved silver scissors to perform the tape-cutting ceremony which officially brought into use Bristol's first flyover scheme designed to cater for traffic demands for at least 20 years.

Before opening the flyover system Mr. Fraser warned motorists that he was considering a 'congestion tax' to beat city traffic jams.

He said he was planning firmer steps to discourage people from using cars in and around city centres.

He said Bristol was a 'go-ahead city' with a great past but it was not living in the past. It was 'manifestly living and planning for the future'.

1965: ON SAFARI IN CENTRE OF BRISTOL

Brandon Hill, a 5-acre hilltop open space of trees, bushes and grassland in the centre of Bristol, is the last place where you would expect to find people trying to catch a monkey. But Bristol's own 'Safari' made headlines when Alf the monkey disappeared from Bristol University and was spotted in the nearby park.

Western Daily Press, Friday 1 May 1965

HUNTED ALF GOES DOWN BITING

Alf, the runaway monkey, ended his five days of treetop freedom in Bristol last night, dramatically and suddenly ... He fell.

An hour later he was back in his cage in Bristol University's psychology department.

But Alf, even if he didn't have the last word, had the last bite

He snapped at Brandon Hill Park patrolman George Hatch, tore though his jacket and injured his arm.

Mr. Hatch of Sheridan Road, Redland, was taken to nearby St. Mary's hospital and afterwards transferred to Bristol Royal Infirmary. He had three stitches in his cut arm.

Alf did not escape uninjured. When he lost his balance and pitch-forked from the tree tops which had been his home since Monday, he hit some iron railings.

'But he's all right' said a vet later. 'He's only bashed his nose and leg. He's resting now'.

Alf limped around for 20 minutes after falling on the concrete path. Children just stood and stared at the 15 lb vervet monkey from East Africa. But Alf knew if he stayed there any longer he would end up back in his cage in the psychology department. So he jumped up the tree again.

Along came Mr. Hatch. He talked to Alf. But as soon as he came within a few feet, Alf moved a little higher.

Along came schoolboys William and Michael Rafter of Oldfield Road, Hotwells. They had just bought a lettuce to take home to Mum. But they stood on some railings and fed it to Alf.

Mr. Hatch took off his overcoat and held it as a net, hoping Alf would fall into it. But Alf did not fall for that. Along came a vet. He failed to grab Alf. Then he was joined by Professor K. Hall with a net.

Mr. Hatch made another grab – and got his arm bitten. Then ... success. Professor Hall climbed into the tree, threw the net, and Alf wriggling and twisting, was brought to the ground.

1965: ROYAL SERVICE

Princess Margaret made a flying visit to Bristol to help the parishioners of St Mary Redcliffe celebrate the completion of the restoration of their church. The massive job, which included replacing roof leading and weather-beaten stonework on the tower, had started in 1961. Some of the music for the service had been specially composed for the occasion

Western Daily Press, Friday 21 October 1965

THE FIVE CROWDED HOURS

Princess Margaret spent a crowded five hours in Bristol last night.

She was met at Lulsgate Airport at 5 p.m. by the Duke of Beaufort, the Lord Lieutenant of Bristol, and a civic party including the Lord Mayor, Alderman Tom Martin and the Sheriff, Councillor Francis Parry.

The Princess made two stops before attending a service of thanksgiving for the restoration of St. Mary Radcliffe church.

She visited Withywood Youth Centre and the Day Centre for physically handicapped persons at Lockleaze, before driving to the Mansion House for a few minutes rest.

A fanfare of trumpets heralded her entry into St. Mary Redcliffe. It was the climax of her brief visit to the city to unveil a plaque marking the restoration.

The church had been packed for more than half an hour.

A quiet, but excited congregation watched the procession of craftsmen, trumpeters and visiting clergy with only token interest.

Exactly on time the Royal party reached the church. The Princess was escorted by the vicar, Canon Richard Cartwright and she took a seat at the front of the church.

The service which was conducted by the Bishop of Bristol, the Rt. Rev. Oliver Tomkins, included a Te Deum specially written for the occasion by Herbert Howells.

Except for unveiling the plaque, which she did in silence, the Princess took no part in the service.

The seven firms and eight individual craftsmen, who had all played some part in the church's restoration, were represented by the architect and the foreman. They gave the church their formal assurance that the work had been properly done.

There was much joy and much thankfulness that the building had been saved and had been restored so well by craftsmen, who so humbly and touchingly returned the completed building to the vicar.

After the service the Princess attended a reception at the Council House to meet members and officers of the church, and left Bristol Airport on schedule at 9 50 p.m.

1966: GOVERNMENT ATTACKS CHURCH SHOW

A modern stage version of Christ's Passion, which was set to rock 'n' roll music and had Christ wearing jeans and talking slang, drew the wrath of the government's Lord Chancellor – although it was co-written by a church minister.

Western Daily Press, Friday 4 February 1966

COLSTON HALL GOES PRIVATE TO STAGE A BANNED PLAY

Bristol's Colston Hall will be become a private theatre club for three nights at the end of the month.

This is to allow the performance of 'A Man Dies' a play which has been banned for public showing by the Lord Chancellor.

The play was originally written for the teenagers of St. James Presbyterian Church, Lockleaze, by former Bristol Old Vic actor Ewan Hooper and the Minister of St. James, the Rev. W. Ernest Marvin.

It tells the story of Christ in modern dress and uses current pop idiom. But it has been banned because it infringes one of the Lord Chancellor's cast iron rules: It portrays Christ in person.

So anyone who wants to see it in Bristol will have to be a member of a specially formed St. James Theatre Club, and buy a ticket at least 48 hours before the performance.

These formalities seem slightly futile as the play has already been seen publicly on four previous occasions in Bristol and once in London's Royal Albert Hall.

'It never occurred to us to submit it to the Lord Chancellor' said Mr. Marvin last night 'We didn't consider it a stage play. It's 95 per cent music.'

After the play had been widely performed Samuel French, the theatrical agents, made the authors an offer.

The firm sent it to the Lord Chancellor in September as a matter of course and the ban was imposed.

But private or public, the play is still in considerable demand. A week after being launched the St. James Theatre Club has 1,500 members who will be able to see the performance from February 28–March 2.

1966: SWINGING SIXTIES HIT BRISTOL

The swinging sixties well and truly arrived in Bristol when the Mecca group opened its Locarno Ballroom. The ballroom in Frogmore Street hosted everything from episodes of television's *Come Dancing* series to pop concerts by the likes of David Bowie, The Clash and The Police. The ballroom was just part of a giant entertainment centre including banqueting suites, bowling lanes, a casino, bingo hall, cinema and a dozen bars that Mecca was building. To make sure Bristol was aware the Mecca organisation had arrived in town it opened the ballroom, which could hold 2,000 people on its own, in some style.

Bristol Evening Post, Friday 20 May 1966

NIGHT TO CROWN ALL FIRST NIGHTS

It was a date to remember last night for 800 Bristol and West Country VIPs who saw the splendour of Mecca's new Locarno Ballroom.

At the New Bristol Centre were the Mayors, the business chiefs and the top socialites of the city and neighbouring counties.

Mecca, having spent £2 million on building the centre, spared no expense in making the opening of the ballroom one of the greatest nights of the year.

There was a gift of a commemorative Churchill Crown for every guest including the Lord Mayor and Lady Mayoress, Alderman and Mrs Tom Martin.

Alderman Wally Jenkins, chairman of the Public Works and Planning Committee, gave the ballroom Bristol's blessing in declaring the premises well and truly launched.

When Mecca selected Bristol for their centre they did not just do it with a pin, he said.

They knew that Bristol deserved and appreciated the best. Mecca had shown a 'swashbuckling and adventurous enterprise' in providing it, and Bristol would support it, he said.

To tell the guests last night all they wanted to know about Mecca, there were half a dozen waitresses, including winners of the West Country heat of the Miss Great Britain contest – in plumes, fishnet tights and bikinis. There were girls in grass skirts who brought on the pineapple confection for the buffet supper.

There was Sidney Jones and his Orchestra playing conventional ballroom music, including an ex-member of The Cadillacs, one of the West's top beat groups, playing superbly competent swing.

There was a glitter and the glow of myriad lights.

There was an atmosphere of rich opulent intimacy warming the place in a way not to be expected in a ballroom capable of holding some 2,000 people.

The night went on into the small hours with dance demonstrations.

Guests were served drinks in the South Sea climate of the Bali Hali bar in the swish Le Club bar, and by check waist-coated, bowler-hatted barmen in the Victorian Bar

Presiding over all this was Mr. James Smith Crichton, Mecca's Managing Director, and the man who hit on the idea of the Churchill Crowns.

1966: BRIDGING THE SEVERN GAP

The first proposal for a road to cross the River Severn was made in 1824 but it didn't become a reality for nearly 150 years. When the Severn Bridge was opened in 1966 it brought about the closure of the long-running Aust to Beachley Ferry, which took foot passengers and cars across the river. For the first thirty years of its life the bridge carried the M4 motorway. When the second Severn crossing was opened in 1996 the motorway from Olveston in Gloucestershire to Magor in Wales was renamed the M48.

Bristol Evening Post, Thursday 8 September 1966

THE QUEEN MAKES FIRST CROSSING OF SEVERN BRIDGE

The newly-opened Severn Bridge had its first ever traffic jam this afternoon - without a car in sight.

The bridge was jammed solid with people – thousands of sightseers who streamed out from the banks following the royal opening.

In the centre of the bridge high above the River Severn there were cheers and handshakes as the English met the Welsh.

Frantic appeals over loud-speakers for the crowd to keep to the footpath and cycle tracks were ignored.

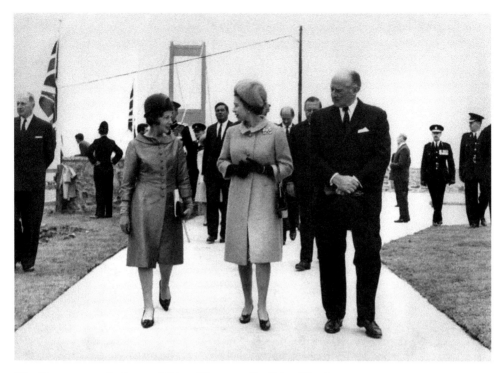

The Queen opens the Severn Bridge. (Photo credit: *Bristol Post*)

Parents and children poured down the main carriageway of the bridge and hardly an inch of tarmac could be seen as they trooped out to mid-river.

Only an hour earlier the Queen made the first official trip over the £8 million bridge to the near-deafening cheers of a 25,000-strong flag waving crowd.

In declaring the slender structure open she described it as 'splendid, huge and technically very advanced'.

It was, she said: 'A memorable day on which all should be feeling proud and happy'.

She said the bridge was an 'outstanding achievement' at a time when we heard so much of Britain's problems and difficulties.

It was cheers all the way as the Queen, wearing a woollen tangerine coat and matching hat, and the Duke of Edinburgh spent an hour on and around the bridge.

The Queen's first spectacular view of the graceful bridge, with its 400 feet high towers topped by Union Jacks, came as she received the royal salute on arriving at Aust.

In all the Queen had 83 introductions; they were not quick. The Queen laughed and talked to many people.

After she had spoken to declare the bridge officially open and the Bishop of Bristol had dedicated it, the Queen and Duke of Edinburgh stepped into their glass-topped Rolls Royce to drive across to the Beachley side.

Watching the Queen unveil the commemorative stone was the Minister of Transport, Mrs Barbara Castle.

1968: CUE HARLECH

Harlech Television went on air for the first time from studios in Bristol and Cardiff with a star-studded board of directors. They included actor Richard Burton, his wife Elizabeth Taylor, entertainer Harry Secombe, opera singer Sir Geraint Evans and veteran broadcaster Wynford Vaughan-Thomas. It had been awarded the commercial television franchise for Wales and the West Country by the Independent Television Authority after its predecessor, Television Wales and West (TWW), lost it after ten years broadcasting. However, Harlech's first night made the headlines for the wrong reasons.

Western Daily Press, Tuesday 21 May 1968

GREMLINS GIVE HARLECH FIRST NIGHT JITTERS

A bad case of first night nerves affected Harlech Television's technical equipment.

The gremlins got in on the act in the first news programme, 'Report,' being broadcast jointly from Bristol and Cardiff.

There were several unscripted breaks and a switch to Bristol for an interview with independent Television Authority Chairman Lord Aylestone, which came over as a series of figures and symbols, plus shots of stars who took part in the gala show later in the evening. Harry Secombe was seen strutting across the stage.

A spokesman at the Bristol studios said that the trouble had been caused by a technical fault which they were unable to pinpoint. They would be investigating it fully.

Television's newest newsman Peter Tomlinson, aged 25, who replaces former link man Guy Thomas, had the job of keeping the programme together.

He said: 'it's all happening here tonight'.

Lord Aylestone said later that there is room for improvement in the standard of independent television.

'On the whole standards are pretty good – but there is room for improvement.'

He hinted at what might be in store for the future when he said: 'We must have some variety and I suppose some quiz shows, but don't let's overdo it'.

1969: SUPERSONIC FLIGHT

Bristol Evening Post, Wednesday 9 April 1969

IT'S WIZARD
Perfect first flight by 002

Concorde 002 had to change course to avoid a light aircraft during its maiden flight from Filton to Fairford.

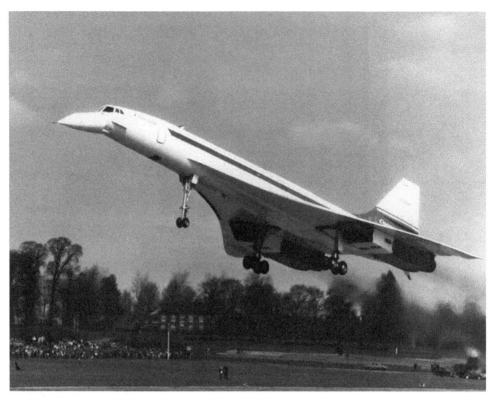

Concorde 002 on its maiden flight. (Photo credit: *Bristol Post*)

The moment of drama came as 002 was within 15 miles of touchdown at the Gloucestershire RAF base.

The single-engine aircraft was spotted by the Concorde crew two miles away from them as they made their approach to Fairford.

The pilot of the light aircraft broke the strict air traffic regulations by being in a controlled zone, and an air inquiry is likely.

The radar operators at Brize Norton, Oxfordshire, spotted the machine, believed to be privately owned, and gave warning to the Concorde crew.

Concorde co-pilot John Cochrane commented: 'That wasn't very friendly' referring to the interloper's presence.

Because of the aircraft's presence the air traffic controllers brought Concorde in on a slightly extended route of about 12 extra miles to avoid any possibility of collision.

It was at 2.24 p.m. that Bristol's Concorde took to the skies.

The years of planning and days of waiting ended as test pilot Brian Trubshaw started up the mighty Olympus engines and taxied to the Gloucester Road end of the Filton runway.

There was a pause for final checks and crowds stilled for the last tense moments.

Then with a blistering, reverberating roar, Concorde 002 moved forward to streak down the runway and rear into the air.

Concorde climbed to 9,000 feet, a levelling off at a speed of 250 knots.

The touchdown at Fairford came at 2.46 p.m.

Concorde landed on runway 28 with a slight bounce and a great roar from its four mighty Olympus engines at a speed of about 160 knots.

Then Mr. Trubshaw released the drogue parachute to help bring the aircraft to a halt on the 10,000 foot runway.

He taxied to a £250,000 silencer unit specially built at Fairford to reduce the noise of Concorde's powerful engines.

About 200 press and cameramen who were at the end of the runway chased Concorde back to the silencer unit in coaches.

Then the gangway was wheeled to the Concorde door and there was a wait for the crew to emerge.

Brian Trubshaw walked down the steps and said: 'It was wizard'. Mr. Trubshaw smiling and waving to hundreds of pressmen said that the whole flight had gone according to plan. 'It was really beautiful and the whole flight was exceptionally smooth. We were cool, calm and collected.'

1969: SAVING MARITIME HISTORY

It was a reader's letter in *The Times* that led to one of Isambard Kingdom Brunel's ships becoming a major tourist attraction in Bristol. Naval architect Ewan Corlett proposed that the SS *Great Britain* should be salvaged and restored. The hulk of the world's first iron-hulled, screw-propelled ocean-going ship had been abandoned at Sparrow Cove in the Falkland Islands for more than a century. But Ewan Corlett's idea was picked up with great enthusiasm in Bristol, the ship's birthplace. A campaign to bring the SS *Great Britain* home was launched and closely followed by the people of Bristol through regular media reports.

Bristol Evening Post, Thursday 2 October 1969

BRUNEL'S SHIP TO BE TOWED HOME

The SS *Great Britain*, Brunel's historic iron-hulled ship will be back in Bristol next summer after being aground for decades in the Falkland Islands.

Mr. Richard Goold Adams, chairman of the Great Britain project committee, announced this afternoon that an expedition will leave the UK early next year to salvage and tow home the ship.

This has been made possible by the generosity of Mr. Jack Hayward, the Bahamas business millionaire, who earlier this year paid £150,000 to give Lundy Island, in the Bristol Channel, to the nation.

He has undertaken to underwrite the expenditure at a cost to himself reaching perhaps £100,000 to £150,000.

The Great Britain will be towed back on one of the longest tows – more than 8,000 miles – in maritime history.

The original aim of the Great Britain project committee was to bring the first propeller driven ocean going vessel back to the port where she was built and launched

by Prince Albert in 1843. However, London and Portsmouth also made a bid to
receive her.

After the long tow to Bristol, the Great Britain will be put into the number two
dry dock operated by Charles Hill and Sons Ltd. who will do the reconstruction
work at minimal cost. This was the original Wapping Dock in which the SS *Great
Britain* was built.

1970: SS *GREAT BRITAIN* ON THE MOVE

The salvage of the SS *Great Britain* really captured the imagination of Bristolians of
all ages. Schools across the city followed the ship's voyage from the Falkland Islands
to Bristol as part of their geography lessons. One businessman charted its progress day
by day on a specially designed map for his shop window. Another even dressed as the
ghost of Brunel. One of the earliest messages about the SS *Great Britain*'s journey home
came from *Lloyds List*, the leading source for the maritime industry for information
about all sections of the shipping world.

Bristol Evening Post, Tuesday 29 April 1970

ON THE WAY HOME

Brunel's SS *Great Britain* is on the way home from the Falkland Islands and there is
every indication she will arrive early at Avonmouth.

The ship, being towed on a pontoon, was expected to make Avonmouth by June 16,
but at present she is five days ahead of schedule.

An historic but matter-of-fact item under 'Shipping Movements' in *Lloyds List*
reveals the ship, her pontoon Mulus 111, and the tug Varius 11, have left Port Stanley
for Avonmouth.

The salvage flotilla should reach Montevideo, the first port of call, by Sunday.

A voyage of almost 9,000 miles lay ahead. If the weather is kind salvage experts
hope to work on the ship during the voyage.

At Avonmouth she will be floated off the pontoon and surveyed before being
allowed to sail up the River Avon into Bristol.

1970: BACK HOME

The journey from Avonmouth Docks to the City Docks in the heart of Bristol was a
momentous occasion for the SS *Great Britain*. The banks of the Avon Gorge were lined
with spectators and a limited number were allowed on Brunel's Clifton Suspension
Bridge under which the ship was passing for the first time.

Bristol Evening Post, Monday 6 July 1970

WELCOME BACK!
Safely home again – to a moment of history

Brunel's storm-battered SS *Great Britain* is back snug in the docks of her birth after the biggest maritime welcome in Bristol's living memory.

People took to the rooftops and the river banks to cheer the old lady on the last lap of her epic voyage – eight miles up the River Avon.

More than 100,000 people turned out to clap, yell, blow bugles, ring bells and fire rockets – and that was only a fraction of the crowd.

I was aboard the *Great Britain* as two tugs nudged her out of Avonmouth Docks and into the river on the early morning spring tide.

A 20 knot wind threatened the tow until the very last minute, but a confident senior pilot Fred Amplett took the vessel and her convoy of three tugs out of Avonmouth's Royal Edward Lock.

The previous night Harbourmaster Captain Tony Gibbons ruled out the tow and disappointed thousands of sightseers who had already begun to line the route. He said that the wind was 'too high to make the attempt'.

Mr. Amplett told me: 'Before yesterday's tow the winds on the night were strong but they were gusty. This is a strong wind but it is steady and that could even be a help.'

The *Great Britain* slipped through her moorings in the Port of Bristol dock in Avonmouth at 6.36 a.m. with one tug at her bow, the *Sea Alert*, and one at her stern, the *Falgarth*. Standing by was the John King.

By 7.23 a.m. she had cleared the main lock and was heading out to sea to be swung around and towed into the river.

It was about 30 minutes later that the only moment of obvious danger threatened the tow. One of the two steel hawsers used to tow her from the *Sea Alert* parted to threaten the whole venture. But delicate manoeuvring brought the Great Britain into the calmer waters of the river where a second hawser was put aboard the tug.

It was on the river banks at Portbury that there was the first clusters of people and a huge crowd that was to cheer the Great Britain all the way down the tricky waters into the Avon.

Pill sea-wall was packed with people and they also spilled from the windows of the bunting-decked houses.

The tops of the huge Sea Wall cliffs on the edge of Clifton were thick with onlookers while car horns sounded a welcome from the Portway road below.

But the real moment of history came as the *Great Britain* slid majestically under that other of Brunel's masterpieces, the Clifton Suspension Bridge.

The crowd of cheering well-wishers on the bridge rained confetti and flower petals on the convoy. The *Great Britain* was passing under the bridge for the first time. It had not been built when she was launched.

And around the corner lay the flag-decked Cumberland Basin.

Crowds packed both sides of the river and were jammed tight across the whole complex of neighbouring fly over roads.

The last lap of the tow, with the John King taking over as tow tug, was handled by the City Docks pilots.

They gently took the *Great Britain* out of the basin at 10.30 a.m. and to cheers and a deafening thunder of ships' horns, the stately progress through the city docks was completed.

The *Great Britain* was swung around at the end of St. Augustine's Reach and slowly berthed at 'Y' Shed when the Lord Mayor, Alderman Geoffrey Palmer, and other civic leaders were on hand to welcome the ship.

A smiling and joking Jack Hayward, the millionaire businessman who made the salvage of the ship possible with a donation of £150,000 was among the welcoming committee.

He said: 'We are all terribly thrilled by all of this. It is obvious from the turnout and the response what the people of Bristol think of the ship. Some were heard to shout out to the Lord Mayor's boat "Keep her – keep her"'

The *Great Britain* will be eased into her birthplace at Wapping Dock on July 19, 127 years to the day she was floated out of the berth to the sound of the cracking of champagne bottles.

1970: HOME AND DRY

The SS *Great Britain* didn't exactly get a universal welcome as she made the quarter-mile journey from the City Docks to the berth where she was built. Indeed, the final leg of her trip home, with the Duke of Edinburgh on board, was snubbed by some city councillors – one called the ship a 'rust bucket'. But she has been successfully restored and is now a major tourist attraction and wins awards from museum and tourist organisations. Thousands of people lined the quayside of the City Docks as the SS *Great Britain* was gently eased into her birthplace.

Bristol Evening Post, Monday 20 July 1970

EASY DOES IT – THEN BRUNEL'S SHIP HOME

Nice and easy – that was how the historic SS. Great Britain inched into the Bristol dock where she was built exactly 127 years ago to the day.

She eased into Charles Hill's dry dock last night with a nudge from two tugs, a heave by two bulldozers – and a shove from Bristol's Lord Mayor and 30 other distinguished guests.

There was drama as the Duke of Edinburgh stepped aboard the hulk at Y Shed in the City Docks

The Duke, arm in a sling, missed being struck by sections of falling timber as a docker hauling in the gangplank put his foot through a rotting deck.

Prince Philip glanced up with concern and then laughed off the incident as he was showered with wood fragments.

But naval architect Dr. Ewan Corlett nearby was not so lucky and was struck a glancing blow by a piece of wood.

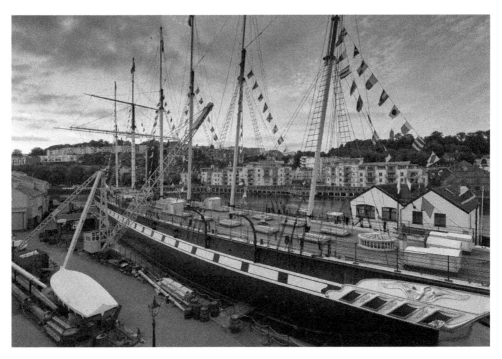

The restored SS *Great Britain* in her original berth at Bristol Docks. (Photo credit: SS *Great Britain* Trust)

There was anxiety as the ship was being reversed into Hill's yard. A towrope from a third tug, the Medway, fouled a rock on the bottom and caused a ten-minute delay until it was freed.

Minutes were vital at this delicate stage of the docking operation since the ship had to be safely in the dock by 9.06 p.m on the full tide.

Then it was free and the ship was steadily hauled in by two bulldozers.

There was then a shout for 'all hands' on the port side as the hull scraped the quay side showering a spray of barnacles as the Lord Mayor Alderman Geoffrey Palmer and other guests stood nearby.

The Lord Mayor, the Lady Mayoress and the wife of millionaire Mr. Jack Hayward – who paid £140,000 to bring the ship back to Bristol – was among those who gave a helping shove to keep the hull clear.

Crowds lined the quay and the route, cheering as the Duke stepped aboard for the quarter of a mile tow.

He arrived by air at Filton and after a welcome by the Duke of Beaufort, travelled by car to Y Shed.

The Duke toured the ship on specially-constructed cat-walks with Mr. Richard Goold-Adams, chairman of the project committee, Lord Strathcona, Dr. Ewan Corlett and Mr. Hayward.

'The Duke thought it was beautiful and in a remarkable state considering it had been abandoned to the wind and sea for 80 odd years at Sparrow Cove in the Falkland Islands' said Mr. Goold Adams afterwards.

The hull was hauled within inches of the river wall at Hotwells as the three city docks pilots, brothers Frederick and George Chapman and John Murphy, signalled for it to be reversed into the dock.

The hull had to be exactly placed to settle the keel on a cradle of elm wood blocks that will support her high and dry when the dock is drained.

A squad of more than a dozen dockers helped with the operation having received special permission to work while the docks are strike-bound.

1971: AVON GORGE 'MONSTER'

People from all over the country and even overseas joined Bristolians in opposing plans for an eight-story hotel to be built on the rock face of the Avon Gorge, just yards from Clifton Suspension Bridge. Despite a national postal strike, campaign groups managed to land some 1,200 protest letters on the Environment Minister's desk in Whitehall. The Department of the Environment was eventually forced to hold a public inquiry. One of the witnesses, Sir John Betjeman, broke into his Cornish holiday to tell the inquiry inspector his views. In his report to the minister the inspector recommended that the hotel plans should not be given the go-ahead.

Bristol Evening Post, Thursday 20 May 1971

'A MONSTER' SAYS SIR JOHN BETJEMAN

Sir John Betjeman, poet and preservationist, added his voice this afternoon to the chorus of protest against the hotel.

The hotel would be 'a monster' and completely unsuitable for such a beautiful city, Sir John told the Bristol Public Inquiry into the £1.5 million scheme.

He said the whole city would suffer if the hotel got the go-ahead. It was 'out of sympathy' with the Clifton Suspension Bridge and would dwarf the Georgian terraces nearby.

It was more important to preserve the assets of the Avon Gorge and the bridge than to support a scheme which would benefit the few people to stay at such 'a monster' as the proposed hotel.

Sir John said he couldn't believe people would allow one commercial company to make such enormous profits, when the whole of the city was going to suffer. He considered there should be no building on the Avon Gorge site.

Sir John dismissed the hotel as an 'old fashioned' modern building. The horizontal lines proposed for the building was 'fashionable 20 to 30 years ago' he said.

Mr. William Huntley, for the hotel company suggested that Sir John preferred ancient buildings and that this had prejudiced his attitude to the hotel.

Sir John strenuously denied this.

He said the Clifton Suspension Bridge was Brunel's finest achievement – and even world famous architects would not have considered designing a building so close to it.

The Avon Gorge was a 'unique piece of natural scenery'. He described Bristol as the 'most interesting city in Britain'.

Artists, actors, students and a couple of Lords have joined the battalion of protestors who are fighting the plan to build a 126-bedroom hotel.

The Lords – Lord Methuen, president of the Royal West of England Academy, and Lord Antrim, chairman of the National Trust wrote letters to the Inquiry Inspector.

And four separate petitions signed by 782 students, 57 actors and about 175 artists were also presented to the Inquiry.

All said the proposals for the hotel in Princes Lane on the gorge side of the present Grand Spa Hotel should be turned down.

Lord Antrim's letter said: 'The Avon Gorge and the Clifton Suspension Bridge form a unique landscape composition of which nothing should be allowed to intrude – least of all a building of the size and character proposed.

Its bulk alone would inevitably destroy the special quality of the Avon Gorge.'

He said that the National Trust feared that if the hotel was allowed, it would lead to 'wide scale applications for large blocks of flats between that site and Windsor Terrace, Clifton'.

Mr. William Clegg, presented a 700-name petition on behalf of Bristol University Students Union, who said they considered the project would spoil the finest landscape amenity that Bristol has to offer.

Artists had their say through Mr. Ernest Pascoe, chairman of the Royal West of England Academy, and his organisation protested 'most strongly'.

The Avon Gorge was a unique combination of landscape architecture and engineering, they said.

Among the names in opposition was that of Sir Tom Monnington, president of the Royal Academy.

The hotel plan which is proposed by the Grand Hotel Company (Bristol) Ltd. has already received outline planning permission from Bristol Planning Committee.

1971: COUNCIL FASHION

Council meetings are hardly the place where one expects to see the latest fashion for women on display. But the outfit worn by one councillor at the annual Mayor Making ceremony caused more than a little bit of excitement.

Bristol Evening Post Wednesday 28 May 1971

COUNCILLOR LEADS IN FASHION STAKES AND WINS A BET

Blonde Bristol Citizen Party Councillor Mrs Betty Topham scored another trendy first at the council's annual meeting – hot pants.

Cllr. Mrs Topham, a teacher, who has a teenage daughter, was the first woman member to enter the Council House in a trouser suit some months ago.

And yesterday it was hot pants.

Lord Mayor's Day is always a dressy occasion and this year it was more so – perhaps because of the installation of another woman Lord Mayor.

Cllr. Mrs Topham said it was a 'dare' that prompted her outfit. It came from an ex-councillor who wasn't even there to see the ensemble.

There was no lack of male admiration, Cllr. Topham confided. 'Quite a lot of the men members were complimentary. Many of them were facetious'.

What did her husband Cllr. Derek Topham think of his wife's appearance: 'Marvellous. I like hot pants. I reckon my wife looks very elegant.'

1972: CURTAIN UP AT OLDEST THEATRE

The Theatre Royal in King Street, Bristol, is the country's oldest working playhouse but for nearly two years it was in darkness. The theatre, founded in 1766, had been undergoing a major facelift. This included incorporating the adjoining eighteenth-century Coopers Hall into the theatre providing a new façade and a studio theatre. The reopening was marked with a musical adaptation of Pinero's play *Trelawney of the Wells* starring Hayley Mills, Ian Richardson and Timothy West. This

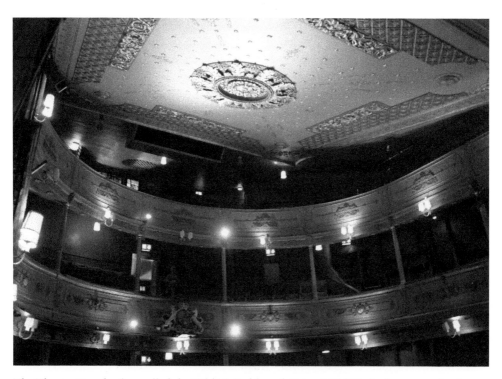

The Theatre Royal, often called the 'Old Vic', although Bristol Old Vic is the name of a theatre company based there. (Courtesy of Rob Brewer under Creative Commons 2.0)

was the first time Hayley Mills, daughter of acting legend Sir John Mills, had a singing part in a stage production.

Western Daily Press, Friday 13 January, 1972

CURTAIN UP ON LAUGHTER AND TEARS

It was an evening of laughter and tears as Bristol's reborn Theatre Royal presented at last to an audience last night after twenty months of darkness.

Laughter, because for everyone concerned with a £750,000 project this was the golden moment.

It was the moment the company, the contractors, the architects, the governors, and the donors had worked towards.

Tears, because it was a highly emotional occasion when the ghosts of the theatre's past reminded us of its great tradition.

Bristol's theatre will go on whatever happens, promised the Lord Mayor Alderman Mrs Helen Bloom, from the stage.

'I hope future Bristolian's will care for it as much as we do. May our theatre always be full.'

And last night the theatre was full of VIPs who included stars of stage and screen, governors, members of Bristol City Council and people who had brought the difficult project to fruition.

They cheered and cried as the theatre came to life again with a sentimental, moving musical bringing a theatre to life.

First there was a prologue written by Charles Wood and spoken by Roy Dotrice which cleverly contrasted the old theatre tradition and the new theatre language of experiment.

And then the curtain went up.

Pinero's play *Trelawney of the Wells*, is probably the best. It is a jolly, touching theatrical piece of theatre that adopts marvellously well into a musical.

And it gives all the back stage boys a wonderful chance to show off all the new tricks that the Theatre Royal now possesses.

There were miraculously smooth transformation scenes, from a theatre set to a Victorian drawing room, to a pantomime, to a row of shops.

1973: SECOND CATHEDRAL FOR BRISTOL

Bristol now has two cathedrals: the Anglican Bristol Cathedral and the Roman Catholic Cathedral of Saints Peter and Paul, better known as Clifton Cathedral. It replaces the church of the Apostles at nearby Park Place – now flats – which for many years was regarded as a pro-cathedral. The Clifton diocese though spreads across the surrounding counties of Somerset, Gloucestershire and Wiltshire. The new church, which is built of reinforced concrete clad in large panels of Aberdeen granite and dominates the Clifton skyline with its three spires, was opened with much pomp and pageantry.

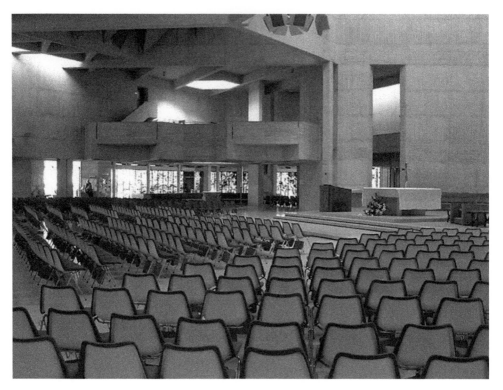

Clifton Cathedral is unusual in that it does not have any pillars. (Courtesy of Ana María Lopez under Creative Commons 2.0)

Western Daily Press, Friday 30 June 1973

DREAM OF DECADES BECOMES REALITY

The dream of decades came true for West Country Roman Catholics today with the solemn and impressive opening of the new Clifton Cathedral.

A veritable chapter of clergy – a Cardinal, a Papal Apostolic Delegate and 33 Bishops – brought dignity and colour to the rich ceremonial occasion.

But there was much joy and applause also as they processed in flowing robes, watched by a large crowd, to the massive doors of the first cathedral built in the West Country since the war.

There the Bishop of Clifton, the Rt. Rev. Dr. Joseph Rudderham, greeted the assembly of gold mitred bishops, knights of the Holy Sepulchure and Priests.

Representatives of all walks of life – ecclesiastical and civil – crowded into the stunningly modernistic cathedral that will serve 100,000 Catholics.

They included leaders from many other denominations including the Anglican Bishops of Bristol, Bath and Wells, Salisbury and Malmesbury, local MPs and civic heads from Bristol and Bath.

The architects and builders, who have seen the £600,000 project through in a record three years, making it the fastest built cathedral in Britain since the Middle Ages, were also in the 1,000 strong congregation.

The cathedral which replaces the nearby pro-cathedral and gives the diocese its first cathedral church in its 123 year history was opened on the Feast Day of St. Peter and St. Paul, under whose patronage it is placed.

In his sermon Cardinal Heenan referred to the description of the cathedral as 'the ecclesiastical bargain of the century' and also to the controversy over spending money on new churches.

A protest group called *Christians for a Just World,* had held an all-night vigil on the cathedral steps to draw attention to the amount of money involved in its construction at a time of world-wide need.

But Cardinal Heenan said it was not easy to understand why Christians opposed the building of new churches.

'They contend that no new church should be erected in this country while there are still families without houses' he said.

'They nevertheless have no objection to new public houses, sports clubs, dance halls and television studios.

The church must think of the spiritual as well as the bodily needs of families. The dog needs only a kennel and the horse a stable. Families need schools, libraries and hospitals – houses alone are not enough.

In our churches people learn how to make houses into homes.

The cardinal said the cost of the cathedral had not come from public appeals but from the generosity of a few benefactors'.

1973: ONE OF KING STREET'S FINEST RETURNS

The stage and film actor Peter O'Toole began his career and gained recognition as a Shakespearean actor with the Bristol Old Vic Company in 1955. He never lost his love for either the theatrical company or the Theatre Royal in King Street. Although he later became an international superstar through his role as T. E. Lawrence in the film *Lawrence of Arabia*, Peter O'Toole was keen to return to King Street.

Bristol Evening Post, Friday 27 July 1973

PETER O'TOOLE RETURNS TO THE OLD VIC

Peter O'Toole, who began his rise to international stardom at the Bristol Old Vic, is to return to the company for the autumn season.

He will appear in three major productions at the Theatre Royal – 'but very much as part of the company' artistic director Val May emphasised this afternoon.

Mr. May said that Peter O'Toole had insisted that he did not want to be viewed as a visiting star but as an integral member of the repertory.

He was making considerable financial sacrifices from lucrative film offers to appear in Bristol from October 3 to December 18.

O'Toole, who had his first professional engagement with the Bristol Old Vic in 1955 will open in the title role of Chekov's Uncle Vanya on October 3.

He will also play D'Arcy Tuck – the Ralph Lynn part – in the last of the classic Ben Travers Aldwych farces, *Plunder*, and King Magnus in Bernard Shaw's *The Apple Cart.*

It will be his first stage work since a brief appearance in Shaw's *Man and Superman* in Dublin more than three years ago.

Mr. May said that Peter O'Toole first expressed interest in returning to the Theatre Royal a year ago and his decision had been clinched when he saw the way the theatre's redevelopment had left the 18th century auditorium unchanged.

'He wanted to do so some real theatrical work again, rather than in an ad hoc company and looks upon Bristol as his spiritual home' he said.

1973: BRISTOL 600 CELEBRATIONS

This was an important year for Bristol as it was six centuries ago that Edward III granted the borough a charter making it a county. One of the many celebrations marking the anniversary was a three-week-long Bristol 600 exhibition on the Downs, sponsored by the *Evening Post*. It highlighted many of the glories and past achievements of Bristol and looked forward commercially and industrially. A highlight was scheduled to be a visit by the Queen. However, thirty-six hours of rain and gales that brought down many of the marquees and turned parts of the site into a quagmire shortened her visit to the exhibition. However, her tour of the city continued as planned.

Bristol Evening Post, Thursday 9 August 1973

BRISTOL'S RIGHT ROYAL WELCOME
Huge crowds see sunshine Queen

Bristol turned out in force this afternoon to provide a right royal sunshine welcome for the Queen's visit to the city to mark its 600 Charter Celebrations.

Huge crowds lined the route of the royal journey from Bath long before the motorcade was due to pass through.

The fact that the programme was running 25 minutes late made not a jot of difference to their enthusiasm.

The focal point for the three hour long visit was the 10 minute informal walk through the cheering crowds at College Green – the first time Bristolians had seen the Queen and Prince Philip at such close quarters.

The Royal couple stopped frequently to talk – and laugh – about everyday matters with ranks of people standing eight and 10 deep behind the barricades.

There was the formal touch of civic ceremony, too, as the Queen was greeted first by the Duke of Beaufort and then by the Lord Mayor of Bristol, Alderman Wally Jenkins, on the Council House ramp.

Then the Queen was escorted to the conference hall to view the charters of Bristol dating back to the 12th century.

The first of several presentations to the Queen – two golden goblets marking the 600 Celebrations – was made.

But it was the emergence from the Council House and the informal walk among the ordinary people that set the occasion alight – and the cheers resounding.

And while the Queen made a special effort to talk to the elderly and the women in the throng, her husband kept the youngsters amused.

Afterwards the Queen was driven around the main arena of the 60 acre Bristol 600 exhibition site on the Downs. She delighted youngsters outside the youth pavilion by stopping her Land Rover to talk to them.

The youngsters representing more than 30 youth organisations in the city had worked day and night to repair damage to their exhibition by rain and wind.

They were to meet Prince Philip but the tour was so behind schedule that he left by helicopter for the SS *Great Britain* without visiting the Downs.

The Queen after seeing a brief jousting tournament in the exhibition area was driven through packed streets to Avonmouth Docks where she boarded the Royal Yacht.

There she was greeted by their younger sons, Prince Andrew and Prince Edward. Later a private dinner and reception was held on the yacht.

It was a day for Bristolians to remember all their lives.

1974: AVON CALLING BRISTOL

After 600 years Bristol lost its county status and many of its old traditions in a round of local government reorganisation. In the early hours of April 1 Bristol became a district council as part of the newly formed County of Avon, which also took in the whole of Bath, parts of Somerset and Gloucestershire. It was a move that was far from universally welcomed. Many people signed petitions calling for Avon to be abolished and the former districts to be returned. One vicar in Bristol flew a black flag from the roof of his home in Redland every 1 April mourning the loss of the County of Bristol.

Bristol Evening Post, Monday 1 April 1974

IT'S NOW AVON – OFFICIALLY

Avon emerged in its own right today – the new home for nearly one million of us.

But while Avon and its six district councils chose the quiet way to come into existence, some of their predecessors disappeared into the history books with all the trappings of pomp and pageantry.

In Bristol the city lost its county status first granted 600 years ago. In its place comes the new Bristol District Council.

At the Council House a midnight ceremony saw the bitter-sweet way in which Bristol City Council held their final meeting.

At midnight a fanfare of trumpets marked the end. The Mayoral chain of office was taken from the shoulders of the Lord Mayor Alderman Wally Jenkins.

For many members the regret of Bristol's loss of county status was perhaps outweighed by personal sadness for they were today bowing out of civic life for good.

The office of alderman ended at mid night and many of Bristol's aldermen were bidding farewell. Among them was the retiring Sheriff, Alderman George Lucas, the last person to hold this office.

Many other aldermen have been re-elected as councillors to serve on the new authorities.

Alderman Gervas Walker, the leader of the Citizen Party, said Bristol was 'a great city' and had 'nothing to fear from change'.

A few minutes later in a crowded Council House local government re-organisation became effective as Bristol City Council 'gave way' to a meeting of the successor body, Bristol District Council, with the chairman Cllr. Jack Fisk, taking over the presiding seat.

Cllr. Charles Merrett, leader of the council proposed Cllr. Bert Peglar as the new chairman and thus Lord Mayor of Bristol, the first holder of the office under the new set up.

Members stood in silence. There was another trumpet fanfare. Then the Mayoral chain was ceremonially transferred to Cllr. Peglar.

The whole County of Avon has an area of 332,000 acres, the biggest district being Northavon with 114,000 acres. Next comes Woodspring (92,000), Wansdyke (79.000), Bristol (27,000), Kingswood (11,000) and Bath (7,000).

The police service for Avon and Somerset is under the control of its own authority.

1977: SHIPS AHOY!

With major advances in shipping – larger vessels being built and containerisation taking hold – Bristol City Council decided to build a larger dock opposite the existing Avonmouth Docks and on the south side of the River Avon. Originally called West Dock – it eventually became Royal Portbury Dock – construction started in 1972 and was completed five years later. Since 1991 the dock has been run by the Bristol Port Co., which bought a 150-year lease from the council. It has become a major port for the import of motor vehicles in the UK.

Bristol Evening Post, Tuesday 9 August 1977

ROYAL PORTBURY IS CHRISTENED

The Royal seal of approval was yesterday set on the City of Bristol's bold move to go it alone in the harsh world of shipping and major ports.

The new West Dock, which the people of Bristol have financed to the tune of £37 million, was named Royal Portbury Dock by the Queen.

It was a proud moment for the men who conceived and built the most modern deep-water dock facility in Britain today.

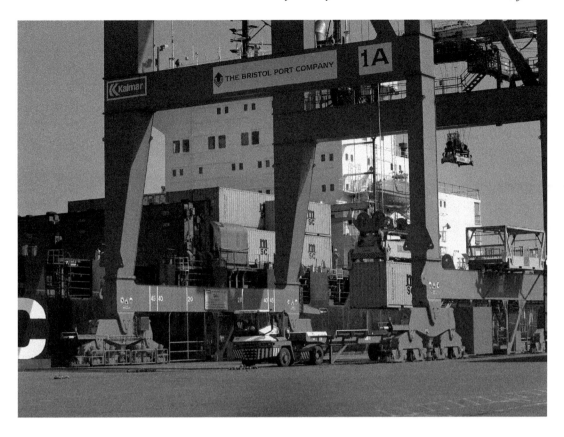

Royal Portbury Dock is a major car importing centre. (Courtesy of Jon Mills, SWNS under Creative Commons 3.0)

There was pride, too, in the faces of thousands of ordinary Bristolians and their children who thronged behind the barriers to see the Queen name their dock.

It was the Lord Mayor, Councillor Ted Wright, who summed it up when he told the Queen: 'From nowhere will your majesty receive a more loyal welcome than in Bristol today'.

His words prompted loud cheers from the crowds, and more followed when the Lord Mayor reminded everyone that West Dock had been achieved without any help from the Government.

Just after 8 a.m. the Royal Yacht Britannia, immaculate in white, navy blue and gold paintwork, eased gently through the massive gates into the dock's 1,200-foot long entrance lock, the longest in Europe.

With Britannia came her escort ship, the guided missile destroyer HMS *Fife*. It remained in the mist-shrouded Severn Estuary during the opening ceremony.

By 8.30 a.m. the Royal Yacht, captained by Somerset-born Rear Admiral Hugh Janion, aged 53, had been raised from the level of the low tide to the height of the water in West Dock. It moved into the dock itself after the opening ceremony.

It was 35 minutes later that the eager and expectant crowds had their first sight of the Royal couple as the Queen walked down the gangway on to Gordano Quay.

The Royal couple were met by the Lord Lieutenant of Avon, Sir John Wills, and his wife Lady Wills.

They were then presented to the High Sheriff of Avon, Mr. Malcolm Anson, and his wife, Woodspring District council chairman, Councillor Norman Haskins and Mrs Haskins, the Lord Mayor Councillor Wright and the Lady Mayoress, Miss Frances Chamberlain.

They also met Mr. Paul Dean, Tory MP for North Somerset, and his wife; the Clerk to the Lieutenancy; Avon County Council Chief Executive Mr. Bill Hutchinson, and the Chief Constable of Avon and Somerset, Mr. Kenneth Steele.

The royal procession left the quay at 10 08 a.m. and drove the short distance to the ceremonial area where the Queen's guard of honour from the 1st Battalion the Gloucestershire regiment, was formed up under the command of Lieutenant Colonel Simon Firth.

After the inspection the Queen and Prince Philip were introduced to the Bishop of Malmesbury, the Right Reverend Frederick Temple and his wife; Deputy Lord Mayor Councillor Jack Fisk and Mrs Fisk and the leader of the city council, Councillor Charles Merrett and his wife.

They also met deputy city council leader Councillor Brian Richards and Mrs Richards; city council shadow leader Councillor Robert Wall and his wife; deputy shadow leader, Councillor Geoffrey Keeley and Mrs Keeley, and chief executive Mr. Pat McCarthy and his wife.

The Royal couple then moved to the main dais to meet Port General Manager, Mr. Stanley Turner and his wife; Docks committee vice-chairman, Councillor Fred Pidgeon and Mrs Pidgeon; Docks committee shadow chairman, Councillor David Poole and his wife, and Docks committee chairman Councillor Wally Jenkins and Mrs Jenkins.

The climax of the West Dock ceremony came at 10.21 a.m. when the Queen unveiled the plaque commemorating the event and naming the dock Royal Portbury.

The final presentation involved dock officers.

The smallest and youngest person to meet the Queen was Nicola Stone, aged nine. Nicola, daughter of Bristol port authority public relations officer Mr. Rodney Stone, presented her with a bouquet.

1978: CHEERS, BRISTOL

For twelve days Bristol became the centre of the wine-producing and consuming world when it staged the first World Wine Fair and Festival. It cost £150,000 to renovate a long-forgotten dockside warehouse and convert it into an exhibition centre. The wine fair attracted 60,000 visitors – making it Bristol's biggest exhibition – from all over the world and put Bristol into the big league of regional exhibition centres.

Bristol Evening Post, Wednesday 19 July 1978

IT'S WINE, IT'S FINE – IN 20 LANGUAGES

The Lord Mayor of Bristol, Councillor Charles Merrett, drew the cork on the Bristol World Wine Fair today – welcoming visitors in twenty languages.

And he announced that the festival is to be an annual event.

'The spirit of co-operation that we have seen in the organisations involved will make it an outstanding success and I am sure it will lead to Bristol becoming an important world wine centre' he said at the opening ceremony.

He saw the Wine Fair's use of the Bristol Exhibition Centre as part of a new era of commercial and industrial development in the city. 'The city means business' said the Lord Mayor.

Mr. Peter Noble, chairman of the Wine Development Board read greetings telegrams from the Queen and Mr. Roy Jenkins, EEC Commission, before the 114 stands with wines from 26 countries swung into action.

The Wine Fair at the Bristol Exhibition Centre, Canon's Road, is only open to the trade today and tomorrow. It opens to the public at noon on Friday.

1978: WORLD'S FIRST 'TEST-TUBE BABY'

Louise Brown made headlines in newspapers and on radio and television stations worldwide as she came into the world. For this was no ordinary birth; she was the world's first 'test-tube' baby. Her parents from Newtown, Bristol, had been trying unsuccessfully for some time to conceive a child before taking part in a pioneering technique being run by two doctors called In Vitro Fertilisation (IVF) treatment. Louise's mother had an embryo of her egg and her husband's sperm implanted in her womb after it had been fertilized in a laboratory – a technique that has given hope to millions of childless couples.

Bristol Evening Post, Wednesday 26 July 1978

MRS BROWN YOU'VE A LOVELY DAUGHTER

The world's first Test Tube Baby snoozed peacefully in a plastic cot alongside her overjoyed Bristol mum in an Oldham Hospital this afternoon.

The historic baby girl weighed 5lb. 12oz when she was delivered to Mrs Lesley Brown (32) of Hassell Drive, Easton, Bristol, just before midnight.

Staff at the Lancashire hospital said that mum and baby were both 'excellent'.

One member of the health department crew who filmed the birth said: 'She is a beautiful baby.

She's got a very small amount of hair and she certainly did a lot of bawling and crying as soon as she was born.'

The baby was just over a week premature and was delivered by caesarean operation by Mr. Patrick Steptoe, the gynaecologist behind the epoch making step in medical history.

Mrs Brown's husband, Bristol railway worker John (38), was driven to the hospital last night and afterwards held the wonder-baby in his arms.

He said: 'I am so happy I could cry. It was just like a dream.'

In fact there were plenty of tears from the thrilled father and one hospital worker said: 'I have never seen a man so excited. He was laughing and crying at the same time. He was choked with joy.'

The miracle baby seems likely to be called Patricia as a tribute to Mr. Steptoe.

The couple's Bristol relatives said that the name had been so widely hinted at 'they probably won't have any choice but to call her that'.

Celebrations in Lancashire were echoed in Bristol this afternoon as relatives toasted the latest addition to the family.

The scene at Oldham and District General Hospital is chaotic. Hordes of journalists from across the world throng the entrance to the maternity unit where mum and her sleeping baby occupy a top floor room.

No one has been allowed in and a security cordon has been thrown around the building.

Mr. Steptoe arrived in his white Mercedes car today and Mr. Brown is believed to be with his wife and baby.

What's in a name? Quite a lot it seems for the Brown's ignored public opinion and decided to call their daughter Louise.

1979: BRIDGE JUMPERS

A Clifton Suspension Bridge by-law that says no one can use the bridge for 'parachuting, rope swinging or bungee jumping' didn't deter four members of Oxford University's Dangerous Sports Club. They went over the bridge in some style for an April Fool's Day stunt.

Bristol Evening Post, Monday 2 April 1979

FEARLESS FOUR TAKE A DIVE

Four daredevils jumped off Clifton Suspension Bridge as an April Fool's Day stunt – and lived to drink a champagne toast dangling halfway down the Avon Gorge.

The four – all members of the exclusive Dangerous Sports Club – took the terrifying 250 foot plunge with only two-inch think elasticated ropes between them and a sticky end in the murky waters of the River Avon,

Nothing had been left to chance in planning the carefully-detailed stunts, except whether the 100 foot ropes would be strong enough to hold them as they plummeted down at 50 mph.

The only practice jumps they had done were from a tree in a friend's garden.

Police and the bridge authorities had been tipped off earlier that a stunt was planned and security was tight as the jump deadline of 6 a.m. passed without incident.

Then shortly before 8.30 a.m. three cars drove onto the bridge from Clifton and the four leapt out. They quickly secured their harnesses and fixed the ropes to the bridge supports.

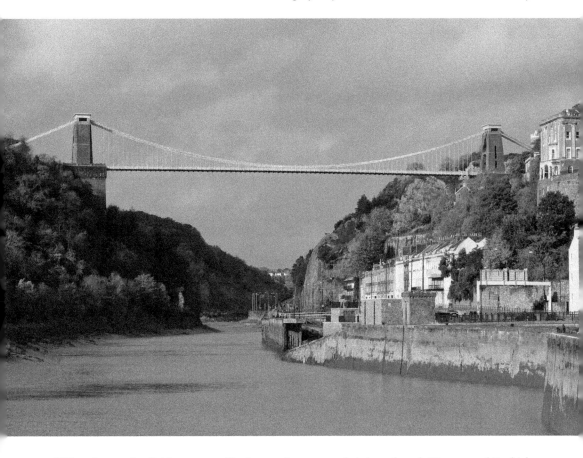

Clifton Suspension Bridge was used by bungee jumpers as their launch pad. (Courtesy of Gothick under Creative Commons 3.0)

Cheered on by friends from Oxford and Bristol universities, expedition leader David Kirk, Alan Weston, Simon Keeling and Tim Hunt, younger brother of racing driver James Hunt, dropped the ropes over the side.

Lecturer Mr. Kirk was the first to jump, wearing morning dress with a topper strapped under his chin and clutching a bottle of champagne for luck.

Simon Keeling (22) another Oxford post-graduate, followed with diplomat's son Alan Weston (23) close on his heels.

Tim Hunt shut his eyes before jumping and then all four dangled patiently waiting to be hauled up as police closed the bridge to traffic.

One spectator, Mr. Nick Barrett, an Oxford student, said: 'They must have bounced down about 200 feet and then up to 70 feet and then down again.'

All four were then taken to Southmead Police station – Simon nursing a bruised jaw after the rope hit him on his way down.

Later David said: 'It was a wonderful experience, very exhilarating'.

The Dangerous Sports Club chose the Clifton Suspension Bridge – Britain's highest suspended span – because nobody had staged a controlled jump there before.

Bristol Evening Post, Monday 2 April 1979

BRIDGE PLUNGE STUNTERS GET A DRESSING DOWN

Four men whose death-defying leap from the Clifton Suspension Bridge startled the nation were today bound over in the sum of £100 to keep the peace.

Bristol Magistrates were not amused by the April Fool's Day leap by members of the Oxford University Dangerous Sports Society.

Before the court were: Simon Keeling (22) of Westbourne Terrace, London W2; Alan Weston (21) of The Street, Chelsea; David Kirk (33) of Park Town, Oxford and Timothy Hunt (21) of The Drive, Beaumont, Essex.

Mr. Ian Dixey, prosecuting, said they arrived on the bridge yesterday morning and using specially made ropes jumped off the parapet.

'The bridge had to be closed for some half an hour while they were hauled back up' he said.

'Normally they would be prosecuted for obstructing the highway, but the bridge is privately owned' said Mr. Dixey.

He said the men were a danger to the police and the public.

Mrs Olga Morrison (presiding magistrate) said the men had disrupted the bridge and been a nuisance to everyone.

'At its best this is a stupid act and at the worse you caused trouble to the people of Bristol.'

After the court hearing the four, two of them in morning dress, celebrated with a bottle of champagne.

1980: RIOTS

A police raid on a café in the heart of the St Paul's district of Bristol sparked riots. The Black and White café was reputed to have been a haven for drug dealers. However, the riots resulted in extensive damage in the area and a number of people including police officers and members of the press needing hospital treatment. A number of people later appeared at Bristol Crown Court on a charge of riot but there were no convictions.

Bristol Evening Post, Thursday 3 April 1980

VIOLENCE RULES IN NINE HOURS OF SIEGE TERROR

Riot torn St. Paul's was under tight police guard today after the worst night of violence in Bristol since the war.

The immigrant district was like a battle zone after nearly nine hours of mob rule.

It left:

A bank and Post Office gutted;

A row of shops and a warehouse in Brighton Street burnt out;

Twelve police cars and several fire engines damaged – including nine police Panda cars which were set on fire;

Thirty-three people injured including 21 policemen, three firemen and nine civilians – three policemen were still in hospital today;

Property worth thousands of pounds, looted from more than a dozen smashed shops; and

Twenty-one people arrested.

Deputy Chief Constable Mr. Donald Smith said today: 'I have never seen such a frightening riot as this'.

Bristol West MP William Waldegrave called for a public inquiry into the crisis, as the Home Office and police launched a major investigation.

Violence flared late yesterday afternoon as Drug Squad officers with warrants raided the Black and White cafe in Grosvenor Road.

As the police took away some alcohol a crowd gathered and started throwing stones at them.

Hundreds more joined the mob, and police had to radio for help.

As more officers were rushed to the scene, running battles raged through the once fashionable district, with brick-throwing mobs smashing shop windows and damaging cars.

As the riot got out of control, police cars were overturned and set on fire, and police had to shield themselves with dustbin lids and crates from the barrage of flying debris.

Police moved in with police dogs and the horde went wild, barricading streets, lighting bonfires and terrorising shopkeepers and residents.

At the height of the 'Battle of Bristol' police said more than 3,000 rioters were on the rampage - faced by 80 beleaguered police.

The officers were forced to withdraw and regroup as 200 re-enforcements were called in from neighbouring counties.

Avon and Somerset Chief Constable Mr. Brian Weigh, who was at the scene, said today: 'The situation was so critical that there would have been serious bloodshed and somebody might have been killed had we stayed.

We were obviously heavily out-numbered and police were the main target of rioters.

As soon as we moved a police vehicle into the area it was attacked'.

1981: UNEXPECTED ROYAL GUEST

Hotel boss Robert Cadei sent his staff home thinking there wouldn't be any more customers because of the weather conditions. But he couldn't have been more wrong. The snow was driving them in to seek shelter and one of his unexpected guests was the Queen.

Western Daily Press, Tuesday 15 December 1981

THE QUEEN CALLS IN FOR DINNER

Mr. Roberto Cadei was quite unprepared that the Queen called unexpectedly for dinner.

Mr. Cadei, aged 42, manager of the Two-Star Cross Hands Hotel in Old Sodbury, on the outskirts of Bristol, sent all his staff home early on Sunday afternoon because he thought the blizzard would keep customers away.

Instead, the hotel filled up with stranded motorists, and among them was Her Majesty.

The Queen's Range Rover was forced back by the snow when she was returning to London after delivering Christmas presents to Princess Anne and Mark Phillips at Gatcombe Park, Gloucestershire, where she had spent the weekend.

Mr. Cadei said yesterday: 'It was incredible. I didn't believe it. All the staff went home, and all of a sudden we were inundated with people stranded. I couldn't believe that so many people would be out on the road in that weather.'

'There were people wanting bedrooms and children running about all over the place'.

Mr. Cadei, his wife, Heather, aged 36, and their two daughters, Adriana, aged 14, and Natasha, aged 7, were dealing with customers when the Queen's chauffeur came in and asked to speak to him alone.

'He said that Her Majesty the Queen was outside and could I put her somewhere while they tried to sort things out?'

After an upstairs room was approved, Mr. Cadei cleared four feet of snow from an outside staircase.

'Within five minutes the Queen was in the hotel without anyone knowing' he said.

The Queen who arrived at 4 p.m. was served refreshments on her arrival and later enjoyed dinner served in the Cadei's private flat.

Princess Anne, and Mark Philips with their friend racing driver Jackie Stewart turned up later.

Had the roads not cleared by 8 p.m. the Queen would have stayed the night at the Cross Hands Hotel. But a quick thaw cleared the ice and snow away and the Queen left at around 11 p.m.

Mr. Cadei said: 'The Queen was very pleasant. She seemed worried she might be putting my children out, and asked to meet them'.

A Buckingham Palace spokesman said last night: 'The Queen had a number of policemen with her. I have no doubt that they took advice'.

1983: HOSPITAL'S ROYAL VISITOR

Princess Diana may well have been the 'People's Princess' but she probably deserved another title – the 'Patient's Princess' – for the great pleasure that she gave people in hospital, especially children. A visit by her to Bristol Children's Hospital was no exception. Even the staff – nursing, administrative and domestic – lined the corridors at the hospital hoping to get a close-up view of the princess.

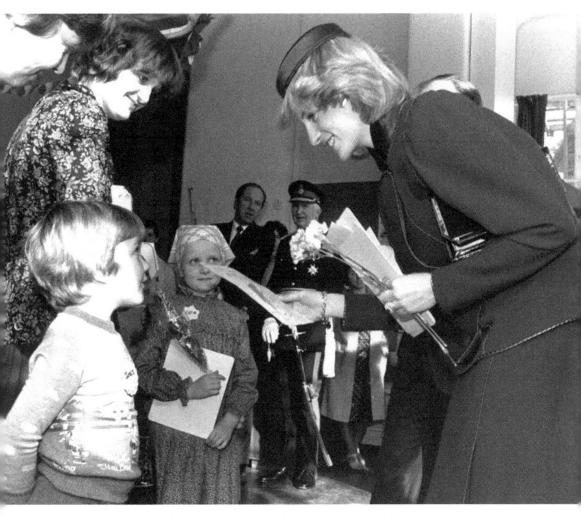

Princess Diana at Bristol Children's Hospital. (Photo credit: *Bristol Post*)

Western Daily Press, Saturday 5 February 1983

FAIRY TALE OF THE CHILDREN'S PRINCESS

Thousands of people, many of them children, lined the streets of Bristol yesterday to catch a glimpse of Princess Diana – the Children's Princess.

She had come to open the new £88,000 intensive care baby unit at the city's children's hospital, and her visit was just the tonic.

The smiling and relaxed Princess, radiant in a dark green wool suit, toured three wards and talked with dozens of children, many of whom are being treated for cancer and leukaemia.

She chatted with mums and dads, sat on the youngsters' beds, knelt down with them at the play tables, and accepted armfuls of spring flowers.

Jadei Castellari, aged five, was one of the first children the Princess saw. She admired his baseball hat with a parrot on top and laughed when he pretended to shoot her with two fingers.

And Dobbie Salisbury, 13, of Lawrence Weston, Bristol, presented her with a scrap book full of poems, sketches, drawings and essays by the young patients.

Princess Diana told her: 'Thank-you very much. It is very kind of you. I will read it when I get home'.

The Princess had flown from Northolt to Filton Airfield in an Andover of the Queen's Flight. She was welcomed on the tarmac by Sir John Wills, Lord Lieutenant of Avon.

She arrived at the hospital in a black Daimler where she was met by the Lord Mayor of Bristol, Cllr. George Maggs.

She left an hour and a half later, laden with tiny posies of spring flowers. She accepted so many that some had to be transferred to her car half way through the visit.

The narrow corridors of the 117-year old hospital were lined with nurses, domestic staff, local authority workers and many of the volunteers who raised money for the intensive care unit.

Mr. Vincent Harral, administrator for Bristol and Weston Health District said: 'It was a marvellous visit and it really cheered up all the kids'.

1986: A UNIVERSITY FIRST

The University of Bristol has a long tradition in the equality of the sexes. In 1876, as University College, Bristol, it became the first higher educational institution in Britain to admit women on a basis of equality with men. It was later the first university in Britain to appoint a woman registrar, and then a woman chancellor. So it seemed only natural that the university's main executive body should be headed by a woman.

Bristol Evening Post, Monday 22 December 1986

WOMAN TAKES UP TOP EDUCATION POST

Bristol University has scored a first in women's lib.

It is the first university in Britain to appoint a woman as head of its governing body.

Mrs Stella Clarke has been elected chairman of the university council and will take over her new position in July.

The present chairman, Bristol shipbuilder and industrialist Dr. Richard Hill, will become one of the university's pro-chancellors.

Mrs Clarke, who has been active in public life in Bristol for more than 30 years, said: 'I am honoured to be taking over this important post and I am pleased to be taking over at a time which is difficult for the universities nationally.'

'It is a great challenge and I look forward to working with the university staff to solve the problems that it brings.'

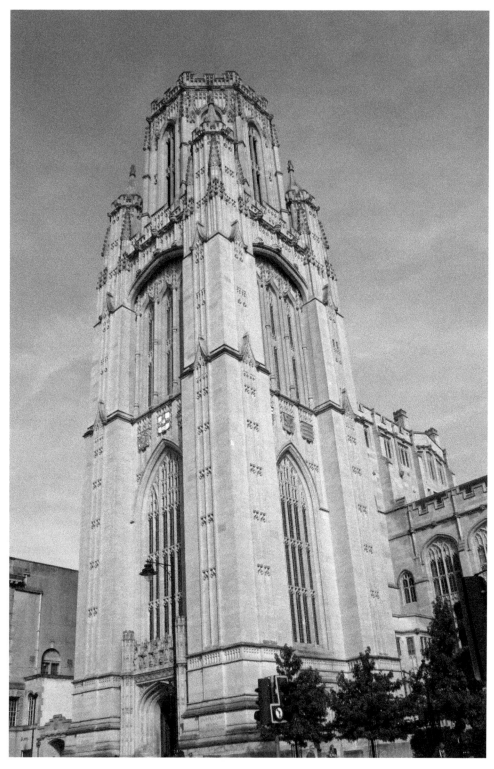

University of Bristol Wills Memorial Building. (Photo credit: Trevor Naylor)

Mrs Clarke was recently appointed chairman of the main bench of Bristol Magistrates and is already chairman of the Juvenile Bench.

She is chairman of the management committee of the Bristol Exploratory and between 1974–1981 was a governor of the BBC.

The university council is one of three governing bodies which helps to run the institution and has responsibility for finance, paying staff, looking after buildings and setting up contracts for research.

1989: UNIVERSITY BOMB ATTACK

Animal rights activists protesting about medical research were thought to have been responsible for a bomb attack on the University of Bristol's Senate House, the university's main administrative block. Extensive damage was caused by the bomb. The bomb exploded during the night and fortunately no one was in the building at the time.

Bristol Evening Post, Thursday 23 February 1989

BEWARE BOMBERS

Police fear the bomb blast that ripped through Bristol University's main administration block early today could be the start of a terror campaign.

The Senate House in Tyndall Avenue, Clifton, exploded into a blue flash just after midnight and Army bomb disposal experts said that a 5lb bomb was responsible.

It was planted in the corner of a bar on the fourth floor of the building.

The blast happened 12 hours after police bomb experts, with sniffer dogs, searched the building following warning calls to two newspapers – one the *Evening Post* – by a man claiming to represent the Animal Abused Society.

Deputy Chief Constable John Harland, said today: 'It was a wanton act by a person, or group of people, who absolutely had no care for the safety of human life.'

'It may be that this crime heralds something in the form of a campaign.'

He warned institutions that the university, or fur shops, which are freely accessible, to the public to be on their guard.

Vice Chancellor Sir John Kingman said the university would continue as normally as possible.

'We will not let this deflect from our purpose' he said.

Forensic experts and army bomb disposal experts were examining the scene today.

The blast ripped a hole in the fourth floor ceiling and blew a hole in the floor. Water pipes were damaged and the heavy plate glass windows blown out, showering glass into the car park of the nearby Hawthorns Hotel.

Hotel worker Mr. David Dowty said: 'I was getting ready to come off duty. I heard an almighty bang and saw a big blue flash and there was a shower of glass all over the place.'

University spokesman Mr. Don Carleton said the violence of the blast was such that if anyone had been walking in the vicinity they would have been killed or seriously hurt.

'There is nothing we do at the university that would merit this kind of attack' he said.

'However, we equally well know that these people act as judge, jury and executioner. The first you know about any charge they make is when it explodes'.

Flooding caused by fractured water pipes may have damaged the university computers.

After yesterday's warning the building was evacuated and sniffer dogs were sent in to search the area. It was given the all-clear at 3 p.m.

Mr. Harland said he could not say for sure whether the bomb was planted before yesterday's search.

'Our sniffer dogs are very thorough but it is a reality that the device could have been put there after we searched' he said.

One theory being followed by police is that the bomb had a timing device and the bombers may have thought it may have gone off at noon yesterday instead of mid-night.'

'A device of the power which was involved here could have killed many' said Deputy Chief Constable Harland.

'The bar in Senate House is not used by students. Police were checking groups that may have hired rooms in the block recently'.

Bristol West MP Mr. William Waldegrave said: 'There must be people in our city who know who these madmen are. I urge them to contact the police before there is loss of life'.

Education Secretary Mr. Kenneth Baker broke off from a Cabinet meeting to visit Bristol.

1994: CHURCH HISTORY IN THE MAKING

Many people thought that the ordination of the first women into the Church of England would take place at Canterbury Cathedral, the mother church of the worldwide Anglican Communion, but Bristol Cathedral was chosen instead. This historic ceremony was the culmination of the most bitterly fought battle within the church since Henry VIII broke away from Rome. Protests continued right up to the moment the ordination service started itself with one local vicar tolling the funeral bell at his church.

Bristol Evening Post, Saturday 12 March 1994

PROTEST AT WOMEN PRIESTS

The world's press descended on Bristol for today's historic ceremony of the ordination of the first women priests into the Church of England.

Scores of photographers, reporters and television crews gathered for the service in Bristol Cathedral at which 32 women were being admitted to the priesthood.

The media circus was in action early for a one-man protest by Father Francis Brown, Chairman of Ecclesia, a society for Anglican Catholics, who unveiled a protest poster which read: 'The Church of England Murdered Today'.

Father Brown from Hull said: 'This is one of the most tragic days in the history of Christianity in this country.'

The two-hour Ordination Service was being conducted by the Bishop of Bristol, the Rt. Rev. Barry Rogerson.

The first woman to kneel before Bishop Rogerson was to be Angela Berners-Wilson, aged 39, who is Senior Anglican Chaplain at Bristol University.

A team of vergers with walkie-talkies was patrolling the 1,100-strong congregation inside the cathedral searching out any trouble makers.

After the ceremony the women will be able to administer Holy Communion and absolve the congregation, privileges historically reserved for men.

Bristol Evening Post, Monday 14 March 1994

CHURCH PUTS FAITH IN WOMEN PRIESTS

History was made in Bristol as the Church of England's first women priests were ordained in the city's cathedral.

The eyes of the world were on the group of 32 women priests as they entered the Anglican priesthood on Saturday evening.

The service, led by the Bishop of Bristol, the Right Rev. Barry Rogerson, marked the climax of a battle for equality that threatened to split the church.

But opponents demonstrating against the controversial move failed to dampen the spirit of the day.

A team of vergers with walkie-talkies patrolled the cathedral looking for trouble makers. But the service passed off without incident.

In his sermon the Bishop of Bristol talked of the 'significant journeys' made by the women.

'Now is the time to rejoice that we have been able to recognise and affirm God's gift of these women who are to be ordained priests in God's church' he told the congregation.

The first woman to kneel before the Bishop was Angela Berners-Wilson.

As the final words of the Service of Ordination were said a huge roar of applause rang out.

Mrs Berners-Wilson, 39, of Clifton, said: 'It was a wonderful service. I was so conscious of the presence of God'.

The service was broadcast live on BBC television to millions of viewers, and the world's press were among the congregation.

Many of the new priests went on to celebrate Holy Communion for the first time in their churches yesterday.

1996: FIREFIGHTER KILLED IN SERVICE

On graduating in 1994 as a firefighter, Fleur Lombard received the Silver Axe award for the most outstanding recruit at her training school. Unfortunately, just two years later, she died while tackling a blaze that destroyed a supermarket at Staple Hill. Fleur was posthumously awarded the Queen's Gallantry Medal.

Western Daily Press, Monday 5 February 1996

HEROINE FIRE GIRL DIES

Pretty young fire-fighter and star recruit Fleur Lombard yesterday became the first woman fire brigade member to die on duty in Britain.

She was struck by falling debris after getting into a blazing Bristol supermarket to check whether anyone was inside.

An injured fireman received hospital treatment for cuts and bruises and was last night recovering at home.

The vivacious 21-year-old was described by fire chiefs last night as a lovely girl who was full of enthusiasm for her new job.

Her colleagues were left stunned, and some in tears after hearing the news of her death.

'We are all just numbed by her loss' said one colleague. Fleur's death, the first in Avon Fire Brigade's 22-year history, has devastated crews at Speedwell Fire Station, Bristol, where she was based. She, and a fireman, both wearing breathing apparatus, were crushed when a ceiling collapsed seconds after they entered Leo's Store in Broad Street, Staple Hill.

A six-strong rescue party fought heroically to revive her but she died minutes after arriving at Frenchay Hospital.

The injured fireman received hospital treatment for cuts and bruises.

Fleur Lombard was among the first full-time fire-fighters to join the Avon Brigade two years ago. Before that she had been a retained (part-time) fire-fighter in her home county of Derbyshire.

Police broke the news of her tragedy to her parents and boyfriend last night. Fleur's father, businessman Roger Lombard, said as he comforted his wife Jane, at their farmhouse in New Mills, Derbyshire: 'We are extremely proud of her. She died doing what she wanted to do. Our only consolation is that from what we have been told, she knew nothing of what happened.'

Avon's Deputy Chief Fire Officer John Terry said: 'We have got 11 women fire-fighters among a full fighting staff of 900 and they undertake exactly the same tasks as the men. We are all aware of the dangers and we take every precaution.'

'The crews' first priority was to ensure the building was clear and they put that above possible safety.'

'The crews were taken immediately from the scene. They worked together very closely and we know they would react very badly to what has happened.'

'All will be given counselling sessions later'.

Fire officers were shocked by the speed with which the mystery blaze raced through the single-storey supermarket which was open at the time it broke out at 12 30 pm.

One staff member in the canteen smashed a window to escape but the dozen customers in the store were led to safety through the main entrance.

1996: FAREWELL AVON COUNTY

Avon – the county that was loved by some and loathed by others – disappeared after just twenty-two years in yet another round of local authority changes imposed by central government. It meant that among many other changes Bristol regained its county status and other traditions it had lost in 1974.

IT'S A SIGN OF THE TIMES FOR COUNCILS

Bristol Evening Post, Monday 1 April 1996

It's all change for councils in the Bristol area.

Workmen were today quick to say goodbye to Avon County Council, which was officially scrapped yesterday as four new 'super councils' were born.

At Falfield the Avon road sign was replaced with a new one for South Gloucestershire – formed through the merger of Kingswood and North Avon.

New road signs were also unveiled on the A38 near Bristol to show the boundary of the new North Somerset Council which takes over from Woodspring District Council.

Bristol City Council also takes on extra powers and the city's Lord Mayor welcomed the changes from a horse-driven coach.

Cllr. Joan McLaren said she was delighted to see county status return to Bristol City Council.

She toured the city with Bristol's first Lord Lieutenant, Mr. Jay Tidmarsh in the open-topped coach to mark the vesting day of the new council.

The new council's have taken over Avon's duties including schools, social services, rates and other services.

The fourth new council is Bath and North East Somerset, a merger of Bath and Wansdyke.

A dedication service, set to be attended by more than 500 people, was being held in Bristol Cathedral tonight to celebrate the civic shake-up.

The shake-up mean thousands of council workers started new jobs today at the same desks in same offices.

Avon Fire Brigade yesterday held a service at its Temple Back base in Bristol to mark the end of the county.

It has dropped the word 'county' from its title and will be known as Avon Fire Brigade.

1996: END OF A TELEVISION ERA

It was the end of an era for thousands of television viewers in Bristol and the west as Bruce Hockin presented *HTV News* for the last time. 'Uncle' Bruce, as he was affectionately known on and off air, was retiring after twenty-eight years as anchorman of the station's nightly news magazine. Yet when he first appeared before the cameras

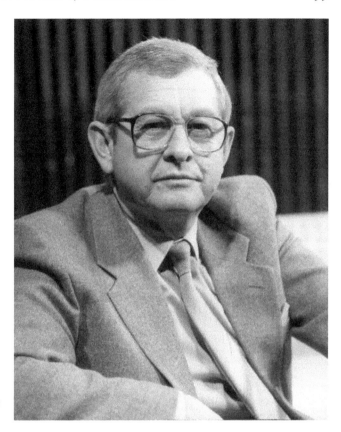

Bruce Hockin, long-serving
TV anchorman. (Photo credit:
Bristol Post)

Bruce regarded the job as a temporary one. He said: 'There was a gap and I was a caretaker presenter, if you like. I had to give an undertaking that I would do it for two years. After that I wanted to go back to reporting'. Those two years became almost three decades. The *Post's* television writer Tim Davey examines how HTV will replace him.

Bristol Evening Post, Friday 10 May 1996

IT'S GOODNIGHT FROM HIM
And hello from who?

Ken Rees is a man with an unenviable mission. HTV's Head of News has the task of filling the voice left by the departure of Bristol and Britain's longest-serving TV anchorman, Bruce Hockin.

After all the on-screen ballyhoo surrounding 'Uncle' Bruce's retirement from *HTV News* has subsided as the end-of-programme credits roll tonight, the Bristol-based ITV station has to tackle a very major issue: How do you replace him?

And, as Ken Rees admits, the truth of the situation is you cannot.

'The trouble with replacing somebody like Bruce is that it is 5, 10, 15 years down the line before you know you've got a winner.'

'For the Bruce you see now, the institution in West Country broadcasting, has taken 30 years to get there.'

'Come back and ask me again in 25 years' time and I'll let you know if we've got the answer right or not.'

The truth of the situation, given the changing world of TV these days, is that it is highly unlikely anyone will ever be able to achieve the long-term level of screen prominence which Bruce Hockin has done.

As Ken Rees says: 'It will be interesting to see if anybody ever has the opportunity to develop the extraordinary career Bruce has, one where he's developed with strong affinity with the audience, a rapport with people at home. It all takes time.'

HTV News is changing, too – and not long after Bruce departs the scene.

Next year they plan to open a brand new centre – a £3 million investment: 'We're going to use the latest technology to be faster paced, a bit quicker with the news to get it on air quickly.'

'There'll be more live inserts into the show and we'll get around more than we do now' said Ken Rees.

In terms of high-tech equipment the big change at this new centre is the world of computers.

Ken Rees explains: 'First there was film, then tape replaced film and from next year we are working in the computer age.'

'Pictures, words and sounds will all be flying around on a computer network.'

1996: SHIP SHAPE AND BRISTOL FASHION

Bristol's Floating Harbour was awash with more than 700 ships of all kinds from all over the world. Tall ships hugged an entire quayside surrounded by square riggers and schooners, barques and brigs. At the centre of the first ever International Festival of the Sea was the Bristol-built replica of the explorer John Cabot's caravel *The Matthew*. This was the ship in which he sailed from this harbour in 1497 and discovered the mainland of North America. It was dedicated during the festival in readiness for its re-enactment voyage marking the 500th anniversary of Cabot's epic journey.

Bristol Evening Post, Friday 24 May 1996

BROLLY GOOD SHOW

Bristol's International Festival of the Sea is under way – and not even pouring rain can stop the fun.

Thousands of people packed into the docks today.

They braved the weather in their bright waterproofs and carrying large umbrellas.

The city is hosting the country's largest ever maritime festival.

Thousands of people ignored the rain last night to see for free the hundreds of ships and boats of all shapes and sizes that have crammed into the Floating Harbour.

Around 1,500 people gathered in wind and rain under umbrellas to take part in the recording of the BBC show *Songs of Praise*.

They sang their hearts out in front of the replica of the *Matthew* near the Lloyds Bank amphitheatre.

And they waited as darkness fell to watch a spectacular laser and fountain display.

The docks are now bustling with a fascinating collection of hulls, masts, rigging and sails.

Visitors from all around the world flocked to the docks today for the opening of the festival.

They can expect to see 700 ships in the harbour from now until Bank Holiday Monday.

1996: A SECOND SEVERN BRIDGE

Thirty years after the Queen opened the first Severn Bridge it was the turn of Prince Charles to cut the ribbon on the second Severn Crossing. It was built to supplement the traffic capacity of the original Severn Bridge and is 3 miles downstream from the first bridge. The second road crossing runs from Severn Beach in England to Caldicot in Wales via the English Stones area of the Severn Estuary.

Bristol Evening Post, Wednesday 5 June 1996

OUR SPAN-TASTIC NEW BRIDGE

The Prince of Wales today opened the majestic £330 million Second Severn Crossing.

He performed the ceremony to mark the completion of the four year project to build a second bridge linking England and Wales over the River Severn.

Hundreds of children, a spectacular RAF flyover and a flotilla of Royal Naval Vessels helped to make it a day to remember.

Two 21-gun salutes also heralded the opening of the three mile long bridge.

But drivers were not being allowed onto the bridge until last minute safety checks were made. It was expected to be tonight at the earliest before traffic began to flow.

Prince Charles performed three opening ceremonies after arriving by car with the Lord Lieutenant of Gloucester Henry Elwes.

Hundreds of cheering, flag-waving school children were on the bridge to welcome the royal visitor as crowds of spectators lined the river banks below to see the opening.

The Princes's first duty was to open the bridge on the English side. As he stepped on to the new stretch of the M4 the Western Band of the RAF struck up the National Anthem before the first of two 21-gun salutes boomed out.

The second ceremony was on the centre of the bridge where Lord Hooson, chairman of Second River Severn Crossing, presented the prince to the senior directors of the English and French consortium of bridge builders Laing-GTM.

The third opening ceremony was on the Welsh side of the bridge. There the prince was greeted by 200 Welsh schoolchildren and civic leaders.

1997: ATLANTIC VOYAGE

The ship built in Redcliffe Wharf by local shipwrights using medieval tools was now all set for its voyage across the Atlantic marking the 500th anniversary of John Cabot's journey. All that was left now before *The Matthew* sailed to the open sea was a formal service at Bristol Cathedral dedicating its departure. Then the Duke of Edinburgh would join the 18-man crew.

Western Daily Press, Saturday 2 May 1997

AN EPIC ADVENTURE

Old sea-dog Prince Philip took the helm of the medieval sailing ship the Matthew as she embarked on her transatlantic adventure yesterday.

But the Prince sailed into a political storm when he dropped a clanger about Chinese-made Union Jacks.

The off-the-cuff quip had faint echoes of the Duke of Edinburgh's 'slitty eyes' comment made in China in 1986 which caused considerable diplomatic embarrassment.

The latest indiscretion came when the Duke, dressed in a smart lounge suit, was chatting to children outside Bristol Cathedral after the service dedicated to the Matthew's departure.

A child accidentally, nearly poked him in the eye with a small flag and he responded by saying that he did not want to be blinded by a 'Chinese made Union Jack'.

Surprisingly he then pointed out to the young child where it said 'Made in China' on the flag.

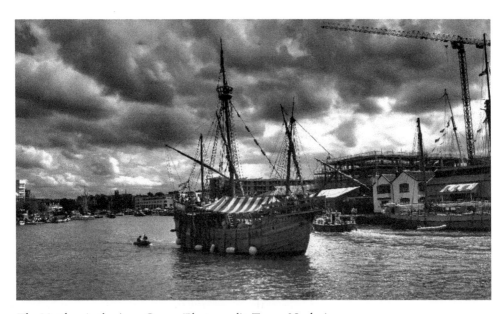

The Matthew in the Avon Gorge. (Photo credit: Trevor Naylor)

Thousands of people turned out to celebrate the departure of the £1.5 million replica of the Bristol explorer John Cabot's ship.

And among the well-wishers was the ship's ten and a half stone mascot, Harry, a five year old Newfoundland dog, and his owner David Pugh from Clapton in Gordano.

'He was presented to the Duke' said David. 'And when the Matthew arrives in Canada she will be greeted by 150 Newfoundland dogs'.

The Bishop of Bristol, the Rt. Rev. Barry Rogerson, blessed the ship and its crew on the quayside. And before the departure, the Master received a gift of a bible from the Royal National Mission to Deep Sea Fishermen. It was signed by the Queen as a 'bon voyage' gift.

The Duke of Edinburgh, suntanned and weather-beaten as any old sea-farer, donned a Panama hat as he took the helm of the Matthew on its first section of the trip.

She slipped like a gracious Princess from her moorings at the quayside and meandered towards the safety of the Cumberland Basin.

The Queen should have been alongside her husband on board the tiny wooden square rigger. But she had to cancel her visit with the announcement of the May 1 General Election.

Alongside the Duke of Edinburgh was round-the-world yachtsman and Master of the ship, David Alan-Williams, aged 42, and the man who put up the money for the project, Cornish businessman Mike Slade.

It was a stirring moment as the Matthew entered the wide calm of the Cumberland Basin, 40 minutes later. She looked magnificent as she gently pushed through the flat waters, turning nearly in almost her length to come alongside the quay at the end of the first stage of her voyage of adventure.

Then the Duke of Edinburgh was driven to the Wills Memorial Building on the Bristol University campus for a lunch hosted by some of Bristol's civic officials.

This afternoon the Matthew will enter the tidal water of the River Avon below Cumberland Basin and begin the second stage of her departure. Then she will moor in the Royal Portbury Dock where a £100 a head celebration ball is to be held. Tomorrow on the morning tide the Matthew will leave for the open sea.

1997: JOURNEY'S END

An estimated 30,000 people headed by the Queen and the Duke of Edinburgh greeted the tiny Matthew ship when she arrived at Bonavista, Newfoundland, in just under two months, after leaving Bristol, England.

Western Daily Press, Wednesday 25 June 1997

MATTHEW'S VOYAGE ENDS IN TRIUMPH
Dateline: Bonavista, Tuesday.

With a puff of smoke from her cannon, the brave little ship, the Matthew, today sailed into Bonavista - forty-five minutes early to a rendezvous with history.

After 54 days braving all that the Atlantic cold hurl at her, the 70 foot replica of John Cabot' s ship of discovery arrived in the Newfoundland port of Bonavista, just as the explorer had done 500 years before.

Well, perhaps not quite the same way.

For this time the caravel with her crew of 19 from Bristol had the Queen, the Prime Minister of Canada, the world's media and thousands of cheering Canadians and a group of North American Indians there to greet her.

And the journey was not completed simply under the power of her mighty sails - but with the aid of a diesel engine.

The cheers of people who stood five, six and seven deep around the small harbour echoed and re-echoed through this isolated community of weathered clapboard houses.

Even the bitter wind and slate grey skies could not dampen the thrill surging through the crowd as the Matthew loomed in out of the fog.

And the excitement was almost tangible as the Matthew actually arrived early - and had to make time so as not to upstage the Queen.

After 53-days tracking across the North Atlantic through fierce storms and unfavourable winds, the ship looked magnificent dipping through the heavy sea under sail as skipper David Alan-Williams guided her home. Two coast-guard inflatables were riding escort on her bows while a helicopter circled overhead.

The famous Matthew 'Roll' was clearly visible from the shore as she beat past an iceberg which had been riding the choppy seas beyond the harbour wall most of the morning and early evening.

Urgent radio exchanges between skipper Alan-Williams and the ship's systems manager, Laurence Freeman, perched on a television camera tower, checked the *Matthew's* progress.

Her mast yard was dropped and her other sails furled as she paused to allow time for the welcoming programme to run to time.

The guest of honour, The Queen, has yet to arrive, and the Matthew, after nearly two months at sea, was forced to turn slowly in her own length about 200 yards off shore.

At last her time had come. The Queen and other VIPs had arrived and skipper David Alan-Williams, his hand on the tiller, pushed the throttle of his twin diesel engines and the Matthew gently nosed through the narrow harbour to the cheers of the crowds and the sound of her own canon firing.

Within minutes she was berthed and her crew of 19 was stepping ashore into the happy embrace of their families and friends.

Mike Slade, the Cornish businessman who put up £1.5 million to fund the Matthew project was there, too, as was Colin Mudie, the designer, and Mike Blackmore, whose shipwrights built the wooden ship.

St. John Hartnell, who as chairman of the Matthew project sparked the boundless enthusiasm which has been so much part of the whole endeavour, was at the quayside as well.

The Queen was introduced to the crew, all dressed in medieval costume, and she received a gift of a ship's decanter of Bristol blue glass before leaving to carry on her tour.

1999: MAUNDY THURSDAY SERVICE

One of the Queen's favourite diary dates is said to be that of the Royal Maundy Thursday service – the day before Good Friday. This service with all its colour, pomp and pageantry is held in a different church – usually a cathedral – each year. In 1999, the service was held in Bristol Cathedral for the first time. During the ceremony the Queen distributed specially minted Maundy Money to pensioners who had served the church or the local community.

Western Daily Press, Thursday 2 April 1999

HER ROYAL SMILENESS

The Queen gave Maundy money to 146 Christian pensioners in the West yesterday – and joined in a prayer for the war victims of Kosovo.

Accompanied by the Duke of Edinburgh, she distributed the highly-prized silver coins equal in value to her age to 73 men and 73 women in a special ceremony at Bristol Cathedral.

The Cathedral's bells rang out as the royal visitors stepped from their chauffeur-driven limousine and hundreds of well-wishers cheered and waved Union Jacks.

The Queen wore an outfit of aquamarine and Prince Philip a traditional black tail-coat for the Easter ceremony, which enjoyed bright sunshine.

Royal Marine's trumpeters sounded a fanfare as the Queen entered a packed cathedral.

And soon the voices of the Chapel Royal Choir echoed through the nave where the Royals took their seats for a ceremony that dates back 800 years.

The proceedings took on a modern tone when the Reverend Canon Peter Johnson said a prayer for 'those suffering in the Balkans conflict'.

But the highlight of the ceremony, in which the Queen delights, was the distribution of the Maundy Money.

Hundreds of people enjoyed listening to the ceremony outside the cathedral, the largest hall church in the country.

1999: LAST ORDERS FOR BREWERY

There has been a brewery in the centre of Bristol since the reign of Queen Anne. George's Brewery, beside Bristol Bridge, was the biggest brewery in the city and the home of cask conditioned ale since 1702. In 1960, George's was taken over by Courage, a national brewer, but it was still regarded as part of the city's 'fixtures and fittings' with the aroma of malt frequently wafting across Bristol Bridge. So it came as a big shock to Bristolians when it was reported that the brewery was being closed.

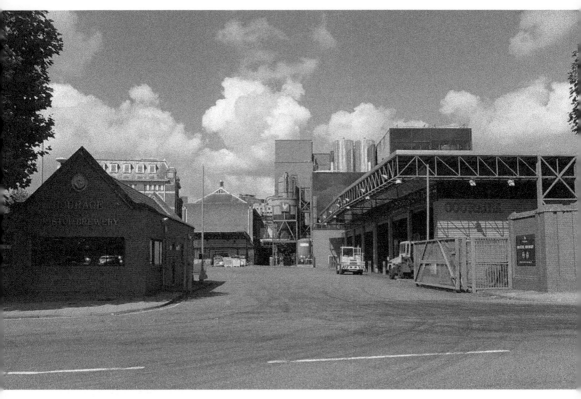

George's Brewery. (Photo credit: *Bristol Post*)

COURAGE TO SHUT CITY BREWERY

Bristol Evening Post, Thursday 13 May 1999

Scottish Courage was today announcing the closure of its Bristol brewery.

The brewery's 75 staff were being given the shock news at special meetings this afternoon.

The closure will bring to an end almost 300 years of brewing on the site at Counterslip.

Scottish Courage refused to comment on the closure but confirmed an announcement would be made this afternoon.

The brewery is the country's largest real ale brewery producing Courage Best, Courage Directors and Georges Ale under the supervision of Head Brewer David Gouldney.

It is understood the firm is blaming the closure on a steep fall in sales of real ale over the past few years.

Scottish Courage is planning to redevelop the prime waterfront site with a mixture of offices and housing.

Production of Courage Best, Directors and Georges Ale are expected to be moved to the brewery's other sites which include, Tadcaster in Yorkshire, Edinburgh and Reading.

Staff were being told today if they were to lose their jobs - or to have the chance of a transfer to other Scottish Courage sites.

Paul Swain, regional industrial organiser of the Transport and General Workers Union said the news was a shattering blow to the city.

He said: 'I have not heard anything about this officially but if this is true it will be terrible news for the city.

It will certainly have an effect on our members, many of whom work there. There is so much history and heritage with that site.'

Richard Brookes, of the Campaign for Real Ale said: 'It is a great shame to hear the news. There have been brewing traditions on this site since the 1700s. It is also one of the last big manufacturing sites in the city centre'.

Scottish Courage has already held detailed negotiations aimed at developing part of the site next to the brewery.

Scottish Courage wanted to develop the neighbouring site, next to Victoria Street but were unable to come to a deal with the city council, which owns the land.

2000: THE 'KING OF THE KEYBOARD'

Trevor Stanford, who was born in Bristol's Southville suburb, achieved fame in the 1950s and '60s as honky-tonk pianist Russ Conway. His playing style and own compositions twice took him to the number one spot of the pop record charts with 'Side Saddle' and 'Roulette'. During more than forty years in show business, Russ sold more than 40 million records and was in the UK singles charts for a total of eighty-three weeks between 1957-63. He died in 2000 and at his request 'Side Saddle' was played at his funeral service.

Western Daily Press, Thursday 7 December 2000

REQUIEM FOR RUSS

Pop king Sir Elton John paid tribute to pianist Russ Conway at his funeral in Bristol yesterday with a flamboyant bouquet for his 'inspiration'.

Extravagant Elton was a big fan of Russ, who hit the charts with 'Side Saddle' in the 1950s, and sold 45 million records worldwide.

Elton sent a bouquet of shocking pink roses in honour of his old showbiz pal who lost a long cancer battle in November. A touching tribute note read: 'Thank-you for being such an inspiration to me, Love Elton'.

Russ rose to fame in the 1950s and was quickly established as a firm favourite with the Queen Mother.

Despite only ever having one piano lesson, his honky-tonk hits made him a musical legend.

Yesterday 1,000 people packed into St. Mary Redcliffe church, Bristol, for the memorial ceremony in his honour.

Bristol-born Russ requested his funeral be held in the church where, as a boy, he used to break in and practise his scales on the organ.

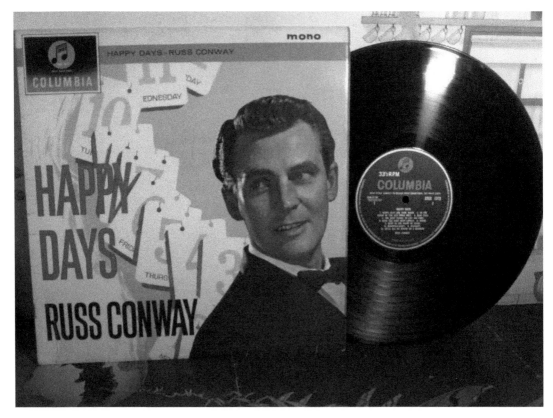

Russ Conway album. (Courtesy of badgreeb RECORDS under Creative Commons 2.0)

During the hour-long service his great friend Richard Hope-Hawkins remembered a 'musician and friend who brought joy to so many'.

He said: 'We are here to remember Russ Conway as a man who has delighted so many people in his lifetime with humour, compassion and kindness. Not only to his showbiz colleagues, but also to his old friends and his family.'

Bristol councillor Peter Abraham added: 'Whenever we hear a piano tune and see a smiling face we will think of Russ Conway'.

After the service the long funeral procession left the church to the sound of Russ's number one hit 'Side Saddle'.

The procession was led to the crematorium by a black hearse immersed in a sea of flowers.

Among those at the star-studded ceremony of Russ – real name Trevor Stanford – was singer Rosemary Squires.

Speaking outside the church she reminisced about her sing-alongs with Russ as he belted out melodies like 'To live on a hill' and 'It might as well be spring'.

Rosemary, 72, said: 'Russ brought many people great happiness and great music. We had lots of laughs and I have great respect for him as a musician. His melodies were true melodies.'

'That man knew how to write and he will be sadly missed, not only as a musician but as a great friend'.

Many people at the service were there to simply remember a man who brought them great pleasure through his music.

One elderly lady who had never met Russ had tears in her eyes as she said: 'Although I've never met the man I feel as if his music brought me something special.'

'I used to sing along to his tunes and he seemed like a very nice man and I wanted to come to his funeral to say goodbye'.

Russ Conway, 75, died in hospital at Eastbourne, Sussex, in November after losing his fight against cancer.

2003: TOP HONOUR FOR MP

Tony Benn's political career, which spanned half a century, began in Bristol when he was elected Labour Member of Parliament for the Bristol South-East constituency. When he took his seat in the House of Commons, Tony Benn was the youngest MP in the country, aged twenty-five. He represented Bristol South-East for thirty-three years and to mark his political work in the city Bristol City Council granted him the highest honour the local authority could make.

Bristol Evening Post, Wednesday 2 April 2003

CIVIC AWARD FOR BENN

Former Bristol MP Tony Benn is to be granted the Freedom of the City in a ceremony at the Council House next week.

The rare honour is being made because of the 'distinguished and eminent services he has rendered the city'.

Sir Jack Hayward, who underwrote the return of the SS *Great Britain* to Bristol, and the former Bishop of Bristol, the Rt. Rev. Barry Rogerson, who ordained the first women into the Anglican priesthood, will also receive the top honour from the council.

The Freedom of the City is now an honorary award with no special privileges for individuals.

But the title dates back to Elizabethan times when it was needed to trade in the city or become a merchant. Freemen had to serve a seven-year apprenticeship during which time they could not frequent taverns or play dice.

Mr. Benn, who was Labour MP for the former Bristol South East constituency for 33 years, said that the granting of the Freedom of the City was a 'tremendous honour'.

He said: 'All that I learnt from politics, I learnt from the people of Bristol. It's a very fine city with a marvellous political tradition'.

He said he couldn't 'turn and run' when the constituency boundaries of his seat were changed for the 1983 General Election and gave him only a remote chance of holding it from the Tories.

He said: 'I could not have left the city which had supported me so magnificently over so many years. I owed it to the people to stay and I have always been very pleased that I decided to stick it out'.

Mr. Benn became MP for Bristol South East in 1950 at the age of 25 and stayed until he lost his seat in 1983.

During his tenure, he is said to have helped an estimated 40,000 constituents with their problems.

As Minister for Technology from 1966–70, he backed the Rolls Royce RB 211 jet engine which proved the basis for the firm's future success. He also fought long and hard for the highly controversial development of Concorde which was built at Filton.

2003: PLAYGROUND PEACE

The national spotlight fell on a school in south Bristol that altered its playground and found it changed the attitude of pupils in the classroom. The government encouraged other schools to follow suit.

Western Daily Press, Tuesday 10 June 2003

School that made peace in the war zone playground

A school that transformed its playground from a 'war zone' into a fun zone, yesterday announced a drop in bad behaviour among pupils.

The pioneering Sporting Playgrounds project at Fair Furlong Primary School in Bristol is now being hailed as an example nationwide and being extended to other schools in the city.

With a £20,000 grant, the site created a ball park, a dance stage, a hopscotch game and a 'chill out' area for quiet activities.

As well as making the children happier, the makeover boosted pupil attendance and reduced the rapid turnover of lunchtime staff, the Withywood School revealed.

Headteacher Peter Overton said: 'We have noticed a marked improvement in the behaviour of children who are now much happier. There has been a drop in the number of anti-social incidents in the playground.'

'Before then it was like a war-zone with boisterous playing about. Football no longer dominates break and lunchtimes. The self-esteem of children has grown and they are more relaxed, more confident and much healthier.'

'After the break they are in a much better frame of mind and are more willing to learn'.

Mr. Overton said the playground also had made life much easier for school meal supervisory assistants.

'Before, they were stressed by the behaviour and left. Now they enjoy working with them' he said.

The school began the project by painting brightly-coloured zones onto the concrete playground and investing in good quality physical education equipment for use exclusively at break times.

A stage was built where children can develop their own dance routines, as well as a fenced ball-park where they can play netball, basketball and football without disturbing other pupils. Another area is kept for activities such as hopscotch and skipping, while the chill-out zone is a quiet area with bench seating and board games.

The pilot project was run by a partnership involving the Qualifications Curriculum Authority, Success@, an Excellence in Cities Education Action Zone aimed at raising standards in schools across Hartcliffe and Withywood, Bristol Local Education Authority, Specialised Sports colleges in Bristol and the Youth Sport Trust.

Government ministers are so impressed by its success they are giving grants to 27 local education authorities around the country for similar projects, including £400,000 for 20 primary and junior schools in Bristol.

2007: DOCKLAND REGENERATION

Seafaring Bristol has been writing a new chapter in its history in the field of dockland regeneration. The transformation of acres of derelict quayside areas has attracted international acclaim. Rotting and rusting quayside sheds that were traditionally storehouses for imported goods have made way for homes, shops, offices restaurants, and leisure facilities centres including Britain's first multimedia and communications centre.

Bristol Evening Post, Thursday 13 December 2007

CHANGING FACE OF HARBOURSIDE

After 30 years of development, Bristol's Harbourside is in the final stages of a £350 million building scheme.

Work to complete the Canon's Marsh development marks the last piece of a jigsaw which has seen more than £600 million pumped into the area.

Shops, offices, homes and a range of leisure facilities mean the once desolate area is a focal point for regeneration in Bristol.

Due for completion in 2010, it marks the end of a period of revitalisation that will transform the Habourside.

Measuring 70 acres and dating from the 13th century, Bristol Harbour was the lifeblood of inward and outward trade for the city.

Sherry from Harvey's and tobacco from Wills were key exports from the harbour, which employed 10,000 people at its peak.

But by the 1970s the growing emergence of Avonmouth as a commercial dock meant Bristol City Council closed the City Docks to commercial shipping. Plans were suggested to concrete over the waterway, with a highway linking Jacobs Wells Road and land close to the SS *Great Britain*.

But by the 1980s a housing boom meant redevelopment was on the way. New houses and flats sprang up at the far end of the Hotwell Road, where Merchants Dock had been filled in, and more appeared on Baltic Wharf where the old timber sheds had once been.

Other upmarket developments followed including turning the old listed warehouses along Redcliffe Backs into flats.

On the water, and at the water's edge, came a series of prestigious events which helped to put Harbourside on the national map. These included the World Wine Fair and Formula One powerboat racing. Other attractions such as floating pubs and the Thekla night-spot, spotted the early possibilities of a revamped waterside.

In the late 1970s came a leisure ferry service, water festivals and other dock-related activities. The city got an industrial museum which reflected its maritime heritage. In 1988 the seemingly indestructible tobacco bonds on Canon's Marsh were spectacularly demolished and replaced with the prominent Lloyds TSB building – the first new major development in the area for nearly 70 years.

Now the final phase of 30 years of development is taking shape at Canon's Marsh marking the last stage of regeneration.

2008: RETAIL THERAPY

Bristol's wealth of independent traders, markets and high street stores was boosted with the opening of Cabot Circus, which offers high-end shops and leisure facilities under one dramatic shell-shaped roof. Cabot Circus attracts more than 18 million people a year.

Bristol Evening Post, Thursday 25 September 2008

SEE SOME OF THE GREATEST SHOPS ON EARTH

Today sees the dawn of a new era in shopping as the £500 million Cabot Circus development flings its doors open to the people of Bristol.

After 10 years of planning and three years of building, shoppers can finally visit the centre which is bringing 140 shops and more than 4,000 jobs to the city.

The fluorescent yellow bibs and hard hats have gone, and the UK's newest shopping development is set to transform the buying habits of people in Bristol and further afield.

Now the buzz of shoppers rather than the hammering of builders will echo around the impressive centre.

The 36-acre site also includes cafes, restaurants, a luxury cinema, offices, apartments, a hotel and a 2,600 space car park.

Bob De Barr, project director of Bristol Alliance, which oversaw the development, said: 'We are tremendously excited to be opening after so many years of hard work.'

'Eight years after the Bristol Alliance was formed, we are delivering the product. It is a long time but still quite quick for a project like this. Over the last few days there has been such a lot happening out there. There has been a real buzz to the place.'

'It is a very important time for Bristol. This is the missing link in the city centre.'

Cabot Circus has a 100,000 square feet Showcase Cinema de Lux, a three-story Harvey Nichols and a new House of Fraser, showcasing the retailers' new vision for their stores.

Work by Bristol City Council to install a bus lane at the bottom of the M32 approaching Cabot Circus was finished yesterday in time for the opening.

Council Leader Helen Holland said: 'Bristol's regeneration and the renaissance of the harbour, the Old City quarter, Temple Quay, Queen Square and our highly valued but previously under-used urban spaces, have very much been part of my world for the last 15 years.'

'Supported by many talented Bristolians and other specialists, who have come to love Bristol as much as we do, we have worked together to bring renewal and employment, as well as spark and new life to our city, without compromising our history and industrial heritage.'

'Cabot Circus delivers our ambition for retail. It combines a fantastic design with the sensible remodelling of treasured spaces.'

The opening of Cabot Circus will boost the economy of Bristol and the wider region, according to the South West Regional Development Agency Director, Ian Knight. He said: 'The city's quality of life is well-documented and it is excellent at attracting and retaining major employers. But the absence of a major city centre shopping destination has held the city back.'

The development is a new beginning for a space devastated by German wartime bombers, let down by post-war planners and – in more recent times – inundated by street drinkers and beggars.

Cabot Circus is not some identikit clone-town shopping mall but a feat of engineering and imagination.

And, of course, the name of the shopping centre was decided upon by Bristolians after the original name chosen for the development – Merchant's Quarter – proved unpopular because of perceived references to the slave trade.

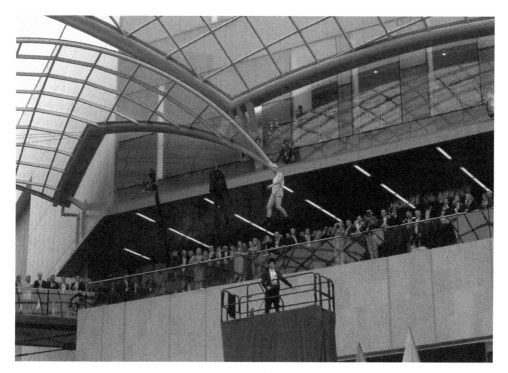

Cabot Circus grand opening. (Courtesy of Matt Buck under Creative Commons 2.0)

2012: OLYMPIC FLAME ARRIVES IN BRISTOL

For the seventy days before the 2012 summer Olympics the Olympic torch relay took place with some 8,000 people, mainly sportsmen and women, carrying it around their part of the country. In Bristol it was carried across the Floating Harbour by the disabled Blaire Hannan, who has taken up sailing by using a specially adapted boat. The next day the torch was taken across one of the city's tourist attractions, the Clifton Suspension Bridge.

Bristol Post, Wednesday 23 May 2012

ALL FIRED UP
Thousands of Bristolians welcome Olympic flame.

Massive crowds turned out to greet the Olympic Torch as it arrived in Bristol.
    They waved, they smiled and they cheered as a succession of torchbearers brought the flame to the heart of the city yesterday.

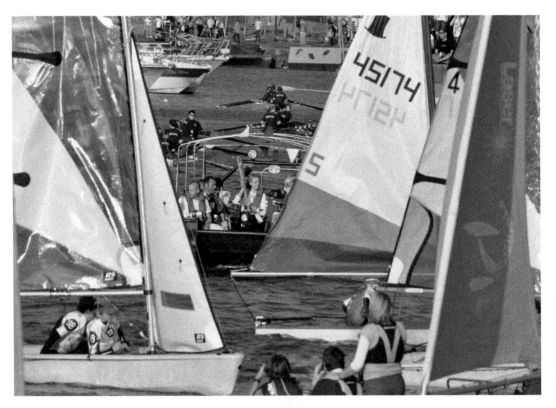

Blaire Hannan takes the Olympic Flame across Bristol Harbour. (Photo credit: Destination Bristol)

Organisers and police estimated the turn out at a total of between 32 and 35,000 in Bristol alone for the once-in-a-lifetime event, with tens of thousands more on the streets between Bitton and Hanham in South Gloucestershire. Thousands more were expected to see it pass through Bristol today.

People began lining the route several hours before the torch's arrival.

Cynthia Lavis, 65, from Whitchurch who watched from Castle Park with her 11-year-old grand-daughter Emily, said: 'I enjoy the Olympics but I can't believe it's in this country. This is something we just cannot expect to see ever again.'

Sam Notley, 36, from Bishopsworth, said she turned out because it was such a good combination of the Olympics and fine weather.

By 5 p.m. two hours before the torch made its final trip across the docks to the Olympic Cauldron in the amphitheatre at Canon's Marsh – Castle Park was already full up with people.

Shortly before 7 p.m. torch bearer Ruth Williams brought the flame to a small boat moored at a jetty at Redcliffe Wharf where Blaire Hannan was waiting to take it on its final stage of the day's journey.

Blaire, 22, from Stoke Bishop, suffers from a rare debilitating muscle condition called dystonia, which leaves her in constant pain.

Her courage in taking her school exams from her hospital bed brought her a Post Gold Star award in 2007.

Since then she has won a place at university and pursued a passion for sailing, setting her sights on the 2016 Paralympics team.

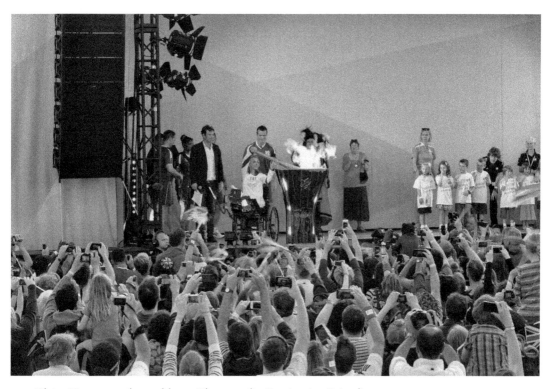

Blaire Hannan at the cauldron. (Photo credit: Destination Bristol)

As she waited to receive the flame Blair told the Post: 'When I discovered that I'd been nominated by the city council, I thought it was a joke. But then when I found out that I'd been chosen to carry the flame it was just a dream come true.'

'I'm just a kid who had plodded along through hard times and what I would like to say is that this is not just my thing - this event is something for everyone. It is just really amazing to be doing this in my home city.'

After her torch was lit, a boat took Blaire on a 15-minute journey to the amphitheatre. Blaire waved and blew kisses to the crowds who lined the dockside cheering and waving in the late May sunshine.

Yacht owners honked their horns, and the bells of St. Mary Redcliffe church could be heard in the distance.

The boat carrying Blaire was followed by 10 sculls and two gigs as it passed by Prince Street Swing Bridge, the tiny flotilla was greeted by sailing dinghies and canoeists, with two hot air balloons floating overhead.

When the boat reached the amphitheatre Blaire used her wheelchair to make her way to the stage with the torch and lit the cauldron.

Bristol Post, Friday, Thursday 24 May 2012

FIREWORKS AS FLAME CROSSES THE BRIDGE

The Clifton Suspension Bridge yawned out of the early morning mist –as elegant and as awesome as ever – impervious to the frantic scurrying taking place all around its fingertips.

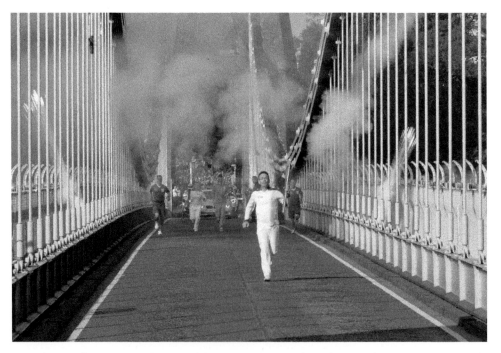

The Olympic flame is carried across Clifton Suspension Bridge. (Photo credit: Destination Bristol)

It was the morning after the night before. What could follow the carnival atmosphere of Tuesday night when tens of thousands of Bristolians came out to see the Olympic flame processing through the city to climax in a spectacular flotilla on the Floating Harbour?

How about an early morning meeting of the Olympic Flame and the Clifton Suspension Bridge?

Despite the partying of Tuesday night, thousands of people were up early yesterday, lining the streets of the city's northern districts to say goodbye to the Olympic Flame as it made its way out of the city on its 8,000 mile relay though the UK.

If anything could beat the previous evening's Harbourside spectacle, the city would have to play its trump card – the Clifton Suspension Bridge.

For Brunel's graceful masterpiece to host the Olympic Torch would see the meeting of two icons.

But as scores of Olympic Torch relay organisers and legions of policemen clustered either side of the bridge and media types and council officials all shuffled into place, most clutching a cardboard coffee cup and forcing themselves into wakefulness, there was an expectant hush settling over the Avon Gorge.

With its road closed to traffic the bridge was eerily silent. There had been reports that a mystery celebrity would appear to carry the torch across the bridge – the torch bearers' numbers had even jumped from 24 to 26 – seeming to indicate that an extra runner was planned.

But in the event the rumours came to nothing – with badminton player Rebecca Pantenay from Cheltenham making the handover in the middle of the bridge to 48-year-old Tom Baker, nominated for his commitments to the health and safety of fellow workers at Nailsea firm GE Oil and Gas.

But the real celebrity torch bearer was the bridge itself which came to life for its big moment as fireworks spectacularly erupted at each section of the crossing while the torch progressed over the Avon Gorge.

2012: FIRST DIRECTLY ELECTED MAYOR

In the spring of 2012 Bristol was one of eleven English cities to hold a referendum to see if the electorate wanted a directly elected mayor. The results revealed Bristol to be the only city to vote 'Yes'. Later that year fifteen candidates stood in an election for Bristol's elected mayor. It was won by architect George Ferguson, a past president of the Royal Institute of British Architects. The runner-up was the Labour Party candidate, Marvin Rees, who was elected mayor four years later.

Bristol Post, Monday 19 November 2012

GEORGE THE 1st

Bristol's new Mayor, George Ferguson, has summed up his vision for the city in one simple phrase: 'I want to make Bristol great'.

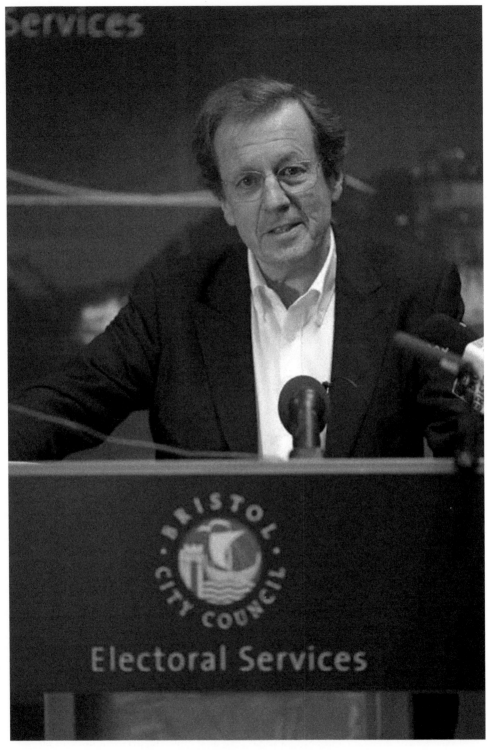

George Ferguson, Bristol's first directly elected mayor. (Courtesy of EG Focus under Creative Commons 2.0)

It was at 3:31 p.m. on Friday afternoon that we witnessed an historic sea change in Bristol's politics.

It was the moment that the voters gave a massive snub to 'yah booh' politics which have dogged the city for so long and elected Mr. Ferguson, who fought on a ticket of being an Independent candidate.

Red-trousered Mr. Ferguson, who will be sworn in today as the city's first elected Mayor, spoke to the *Post* outside the Council House which he wants to call 'City Hall' to reflect its role as a 'democratic marketplace' for the people of Bristol.

He said there were two main ways for the city to achieve greatness.

First, it meant going out to the rest of the world and making sure everyone recognised Bristol's great qualities, and secondly that people felt a sense of pride in the city.

He said the richness of the people, the city's diversity and innovation and skill, made it the best city outside London for investment.

He added: 'It is just as important that people feel proud of their city. There has been a certain amount of cynicism which has been shown with the turnout at the election and I hope by the end of this three-and-and-a-half year term that we have got a population that really feels a part of the city and it is recognised from City Hall that they are important.

Final result: George Ferguson (Bristol 1st) 37,353 votes; Marvin Rees (Labour) 31,259 votes. Turnout: 28%

2013: RUGBY CLUB TRYING FOR FIRST HOME WIN

Bristol Post, Thursday 26 September 2013

RUGBY'S COMING HOME AT LONG LAST FOR CLIFTON RFC

They were founded in Clifton, named after Clifton and now, after a 141 year wait, Clifton RFC will, at last, play their first game as the home side actually in Clifton.

In 1872, a notice was circulated among residents and on September 27, at the Kings Arms on Blackboy Hill in Clifton, 20 hardy souls met and Clifton Rugby Club was formed.

But while it is the oldest club in the city it has led a somewhat nomadic existence playing in Redland, Horfield, Westbury-on-Trym and most recently Cribbs Causeway but never finding a base in its place of origin.

The club until the early 1970s used to play Clifton College due to its ongoing close ties with the school, but they were always the away side at the Clifton Close Ground.

But this weekend the players chosen to pull on the club shirt will proudly run out at Clifton College for their league match with Bishops Stortford as the home side after an agreement with the school's headmaster was struck.

And Clifton, the current SSE National League 2 South leaders will hope to do the fixture justice by beating the visitors who are currently languishing behind them in ninth.

The significance of the fixture is underlined by the fact RFU president Bob Reeves, a former backs coach, at Bristol RFC, will attend.

Darren Lloyd, Clifton RFC Director of Rugby, said: 'We have the opportunity to play a historic game on a great pitch and fabulous location.'

'I have walked from the changing rooms in the cricket pavilion to the school's first team pitch and it made the hairs on the back of my neck stand up. It's an awesome venue.'

'That message has filtered back to the players and they all want to be part of the occasion.'

'We have had a good start to the season so competition for places is already fierce but this game has certainly added a little edge to training because everybody wants to be part of what is going to be part of the club's rich history.'

The club's commercial director, Jamie Farrell, said the club was very excited about the game which they hope will become an annual event. He even went as far as likening it to Saracens playing a game at Wembley.

'The players are very excited about it' he said.

'The team will be announced this evening and the players will be presented with their match day shirt'.

The shirt in itself is special this season after someone found a velvet cap with a crest that has been transferred as accurately as possible onto the new club shirt.

'It's a very special occasion in an amazing setting' Mr. Farrell added.

'We have always had close ties with the college and a lot of our supporters are from Clifton so in a strange way it feels like a home coming even though it has never been home.'

'Up until the late 1960s, early 1970s we were playing against Clifton College and we were very much the away team.'

'This time we will be playing in the grounds of Clifton College as the home team – and something we have never done in our 141 year existence.'

'In that sense it's a very historic occasion and having the President of the RFU in attendance is testament to that' said Mr. Farrell.

Clifton RFC has a rich history of producing quality players who have gone on to represent their countries and prides itself on its thriving mini and junior sections.

One of the latest players to do the club proud is Mako Vunipola. Just four years ago he was playing for Clifton before moving on to Bristol RFC and then Saracens and England.

The explosive prop then exceeded all expectations by winning a place on the British Lions tour to Australia earlier this year and playing his part in a 2-1 series victory.

2015: BUSINESS AND THE CLASSROOM

All over Bristol business people are volunteering to go back to the classroom, not to brush up on their English or maths but as number partners, reading buddies or mentors. More than 1,400 pupils in primary schools across the city are receiving extra help from these business volunteers. They have signed up with the Bristol education charity Ablaze – A Bristol Learning Action Zone for Education – which organises one-to-one support from the volunteers who visit classrooms on a regular basis. Now the charity has been honoured with a prestigious royal award in recognition of its work over the last ten years.

Bristol Post, Wednesday 23 December 2015

ROYAL RECOGNITION FOR BUSINESS VOLUNTEERS

A charity which connects business with education received royal recognition for its work.

Ablaze was presented with the Queen's Award for Voluntary Service by the Lord Lieutenant of the City and County of Bristol, Mrs Mary Prior.

The award is the highest honour given to voluntary groups across the UK and is regarded as the MBE for voluntary and charitable sectors.

The charity was founded in 2005 with the goal of raising attainment and aspiration among Bristol children. It helps businesses and schools form partnerships with activities such as reading buddies, mentoring and mock interviews.

Roger Opie, outgoing chief executive at the charity, said: 'The Queen's Award for Voluntary Service must be attributed to our dedicated trustees, enthusiastic staff, responsive young people and welcoming schools but above all the business volunteers who give their time generously. They work with passion and commitment to benefit young people.'

Co-founding trustees Nigel Hutchings and Malcolm Broad, who have remained supportive of its work, said: 'The success in both primary and secondary schools has been astonishing with huge business engagement of volunteers going into schools every week.'

'The trustees are hugely grateful for the support provided by Bristol City Council, numerous employers, schools and young people'.

2016: MASSIVE CONCERT

More than 27,000 people descended on Clifton and Durdham Downs – 400 odd acres of grassland and woodland in the north-west of the city – but not for its natural history. They were there for the biggest event the Downs has held in fifteen years: an open-air concert by Massive Attack. Tickets to see this trip hop group formed in 1988 in Bristol sold out months before the event and this mini-festival turned out to be a huge success.

Bristol Post, Monday 5 September 2016

MASSIVE GIG MAKES HISTORY ON THE DOWNS

The first hometown gig in 11 years for Bristol's biggest musical export was always going to be special and Massive Attack's mini-festival on The Downs is already assured a place in the city's musical history.

For a band so synonymous with what is known globally as 'the Bristol sound' it's easy to forget just how rare Massive Attack performances are.

In 25 years they have only played Bristol a handful of times since their legendary first live show at Ashton Court Mansion and this was their biggest gig on home soil since Queen Square in 2003, if you discount their brief appearance alongside Portishead at the Tsunami in Asia benefit gig at the 02 Academy in 2005.

By the time Massive Attack appeared, monsoon-like rain was soaking the 27,000 fans surrounding the main stage close to the Sea Walls alongside the Avon Gorge.

With the stage cloaked in darkness and the rain now virtually horizontal, the band finally appeared to the unmistakable rumbling bass lines of *Hymn of The Big Wheel* – the first of several songs from the band's seminal first album, *Blue Lines*, which is currently celebrating its 25th anniversary.

It marked the first appearance of the night for veteran reggae singer Horace Andy, whose haunting, fragile vocals pierced the spliff-heavy air. Andy returned soon after for 'Man Next Door and Girl I love You'.

Over the course of 90 rain-swept minutes, Massive Attack mined their 25-year back catalogue, revisiting songs from *Blue Lines*, but also the albums *Mezzanine*, *Heligoland*, *Protection* and *100th Window*.

As with any Massive Attack performance, founder members Robert Del Naja (3D) and Grant Marshall (Daddy G) were the anchormen, alongside long-serving musicians like the brilliantly gifted guitarist Angelo Bruschini.

For the most part 3D and Daddy G kept a low profile in the background as a procession of guest vocalists filed on and off the stage.

After Horace Andy, it was the turn of London singer Azekel for *Ritual Spirit*, and then Edinburgh hip hop trio The Young Fathers performed four songs, including their own anthem 'Shame' from their award-winning album (*White Men Are Black Men Too)* and their Massive Attack collaboration *Voodoo In My Blood*.

But it wasn't just songs performed by guest vocalists that stood out. Against a backdrop of head-spinning digital data, 3D took the mic for a brilliant version of 'Future Proof' and a rare live outing for 'Eurochild', introduced as 'a song written 20 years ago as a requiem to the EU'.

3D returned to the mic for 'Inertia Creeps' and the closing half hour of back-to-back crowd pleasers, kicking off with the final appearance of Horace Andy for the classic 'Angel', which generated one of the biggest cheers and mass dance-alongs of the evening.

If there was a defining Bristol moment of the show it had to be the arrival of Tricky on stage. 'I'm home, I'm home' grinned the rapper, who these days spends more time in New York than his original home of Knowle West, although the throbbing bass for 'Take It There' was probably felt as far as the south Bristol council estate where he grew up.

Tricky reunited with Massive Attack on home turf was very much a Bristol moment to behold, although it was a shame he only appeared for one song and surprising they didn't dust off the better-known *Karmacoma* for the occasion.

It also gave 3D – once a well-known spray can figure in Bristol – the opportunity to address the rumours that he was really Banksy, joking first that Tricky was the elusive graffiti artist before saying 'actually, we are all Banksy', a headline-grabbing quote which could be open to even more speculation and interpretation.

It was left to ace soul diva Deborah Miller to leave a final lasting impression with her mighty vocal on the anthemic 'Safe From Harm' and the predictable encore of 'Unfinished Symphony' – two of Massive Attack's best-loved and iconic tracks from *Blue Lines*.

'Thank-you so much, this has been mind blowing' shouted Daddy G as the lights were turned up at the end of the evening, with 3D thanking the organisers for making it happen on The Downs and thanking the fans for buying the tickets so quickly.

As shows go, it wasn't perfect and there will be some who might feel the set (which was essentially the same one they have been playing at festivals around Europe all summer) didn't contain enough surprises for such a long-awaited and anticipated home-coming.

But despite all of this and despite the torrential rain and the serious problems with bar queues and the like, Massive Attack on The Downs will go down in history as one of the rare 'I was there' moments and the 27,000 people who did brave the appalling weather will be talking about it for several years to come.

2016: CYCLING CITY

Lots of people laughed when the government made Bristol the first 'Cycling City' in England in 2008, giving it £11 million to encourage more cycling. After all Bristol was a city built on some rather steep hills. But it had the last laugh for both in 2014 and 2016 Bristol was chosen for one of the stages of the Tour of Britain cycle race. In 2016, the world's cycling elite had to tackle a course that included Bridge Valley Road for the King of the Mountains climb. The road rises from around 30 feet above sea level to 245 feet.

Bristol Post, Monday 12 September 2016

CYCLING TOUR HAS BROUGHT IN £3 MILLION

About £3 million was spent by visitors to Bristol's Tour of Britain stage on Saturday and live coverage worldwide will keep the benefits coming, sport and tourism leaders say.

It is estimated about 150,000 people turned out to watch stage seven of the tour – a 15km circuit beginning on the Downs and taking in beauty spots like Clifton Suspension Bridge.

The global coverage has also sown seeds for people to visit Bristol and give an extra boost to tourism in the city.

An earlier count said stage seven, won by Australian Rohan Dennis, clocked up 100,000 spectators but Bristol Sports Partnership chairman Colin Sexstone said it was closer to 150,000.

'There's no doubt about that – it was a huge number of people and the atmosphere was tremendous, both up on the Downs and all around the route' he said.

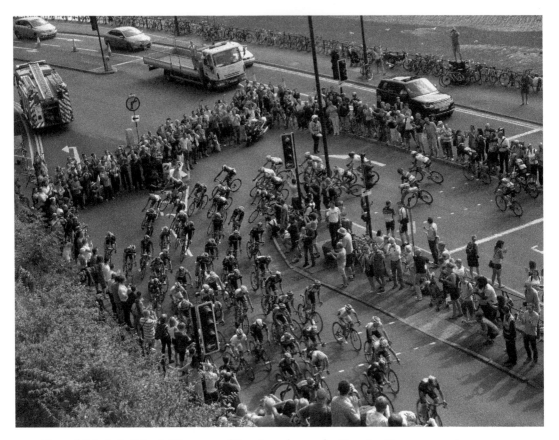

Tour of Britain in Bristol. (Courtesy of Sam Saunders under Creative Commons 2.0)

'It just shows the interest Bristol has in sport in general and cycling specifically, so that is tremendous.'

Tour bosses will put an official figure on attendance and money generated, but Mr. Sexstone said a 'conservative' guess was it boosted Bristol's economy by £3 million.

Mr. Sexstone added that about 20 per cent of spectators were from outside the city, spending cash on hotels, restaurants and transport.

'It could be more' he said.

'The other thing you can never put a figure on is it was live on ITV and it showed Bristol in the most wonderful way. How many of those viewers will then come to Bristol one can never know. It was a tremendous advert for Bristol'.

The day had started wet and grey, but that faded soon after the time trials, which began at 10 a.m. and the sun was out when the main race started at 2.30 p.m.

John Hirst, chief executive of Destination Bristol, said: 'Crowds just flocked out. We were delighted and it exceeded our expectations. They were three or four deep at some stages.'

'We always hoped it would bring economic benefits to the whole city and the tour touched different parts of the city. We wanted it to have a positive impact everywhere.'

'We worked with the tour organisers to try and give them information about the city and they used it. For me it's sown seeds in people's minds to come and look at this fabulous city.'

The Tour of Britain entered its final stage yesterday, as riders competed in a circuit through the centre of London.

2017: CONCORDE GETS A HOME

After making a farewell flight in 2003 over Brunel's Clifton Suspension Bridge in Bristol – watched by many thousands of people – the last Concorde to be built at Filton flew back to its birthplace. Since then Concorde 216 has stood on the runway while discussions have been taking place about a permanent home for the aircraft. Then in early 2017, completely unannounced by the aircraft authorities, Concorde was on the move again ... this time at walking pace. It was towed to the new Aviation Centre being built on the other side of the Filton runway.

Bristol Post, Wednesday 8 February 2017

AFTER 13 YEARS ON THE RUNWAY, CONCORDE MOVES INO NEW HOME

After standing forlornly on the runway at Filton Airfield for the past 13 years, Concorde has at last been given a new home.

Watched by a small group of aircraft enthusiasts and journalists, she was towed at walking pace from the far side of the runway to take pride of place in the new £19 million Aviation Centre which is now being built on the other side of the airfield near Cribbs Causeway.

The journey only took about an hour. Part of the hangar where she will reside was removed so she could be wheeled into place.

Concorde 216 was the last of the iconic supersonic planes to be built and the last to fly.

Thousands of people turned out to watch her land at Filton on 26 November 2003 after a fly-past over the Clifton Suspension Bridge.

Concorde first flew commercial flights in 1976 and they ended 27 years later in October 2003.

Several of the world's major airlines were expected to place orders for the supersonic plane but there was a lack of enthusiasm due to environmental factors, worries about the plane's sonic boom and the operating costs.

Concorde could travel at more than twice the speed of sound (mach 2.0 or about 1,520mph) and when she broke the sound barrier, the sonic boom sounded like a loud bang, crack or deep rumble.

She could also fly much higher than conventional planes, mostly at 50–55,000 feet but at 60,000 feet, you were at the edge of space which meant you could see the curvature of earth.

The supersonic plane recorded its fastest journey from New York to London on 1 January 1983, taking two hours 56 minutes.

She was considered the safest aircraft in the world until 25 July 2000, when one of the planes belonging to Air France crashed shortly after taking off from Paris, killing 113 people.

It later emerged that debris from a punctured tyre ruptured the fuel tank.

The new Aviation Centre will be more than just a home for Concorde 216. It will also house the Bristol Aero Collection of aviation artefacts as well as provide an educational centre for budding aviation engineers.

The new centre, which includes the renovation of listed hangars which were built during the First World War, is due to open in summer. 2017.

2017: FIRST BLACK LORD LIEUTENANT

Peaches Golding belongs to one of the most exclusive clubs in the land. There are only ninety-eight members and all have the title of Her Majesty's Lord Lieutenant. Not only is Peaches the Queen's personal representative in Bristol but it's believed she's the first black woman to hold such a post in the country.

Bristol Post, Tuesday 7 March 2017

PEACHES MAKES HISTORY WITH ROLE AS NEW LORD LIEUTENANT

Peaches Golding is believed to have made history by becoming the first black woman in the country to become a Lord Lieutenant.

Her role as Lord Lieutenant of Bristol will be to represent the Queen at major events and functions in the city and promote a spirit of co-operation and goodwill.

American-born Peaches, 64, a former High Sheriff in the city, said it was a 'huge privilege' to have been chosen for the ceremonial post.

She added: 'I think in terms of where I came from to get this is just amazing.'

'I've lived and worked in Bristol for 35 years and very much taken Bristol to my heart so this means an enormous amount to me.'

As a black woman to hold this post, she said it was for other people to decide whether she was a role model.

'I came from an ordinary background and if I can inspire people to do extraordinary things, then that makes me very happy' she said.

Peaches takes over from Mary Prior, who retires from the post on her 75th birthday next month.

She said: 'I would really like to see Bristol proud of what we have achieved and what we can do.'

'I hope a light can be shone on the tremendous work in Bristol, both in the voluntary and business sectors'.

Peaches, who was born in South Carolina, worked as a teacher in Nigeria after graduating and set up a marketing and communications business in Bristol in 1992.

Her father, Charles Hauser, took on the American Greyhound bus company in 1947 and won a settlement after he was arrested for refusing to move to the back of a bus.

Peaches has held many public and charitable posts during her years in Bristol and the only known black High Sheriff of England, another ceremonial post which was established more than 1,000years ago.

In 2009 she was awarded the OBE for services to minority ethnic people in the south west.

She lives in Leigh Woods with her husband Bob, a retired zoologist.

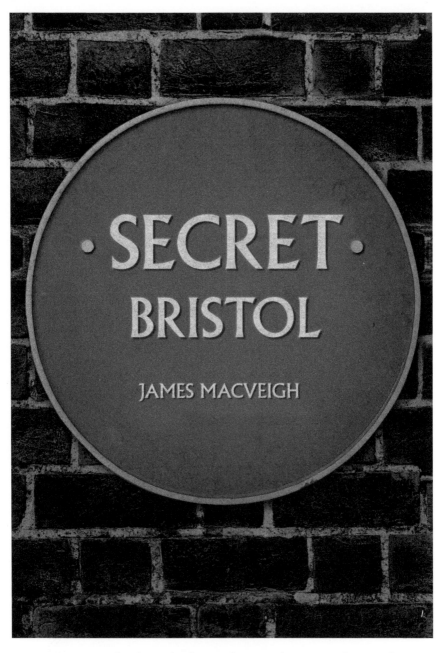